The Seed Saving Bible [7 Books in 1]

Harvest, Store, Germinate and Keep Plants,
Vegetables, Fruits, Herbs Fresh for Years,
Build Your Seed Bank & Become a Seed Master.
Perfect for Modern Preppers

by

Steven Dowding

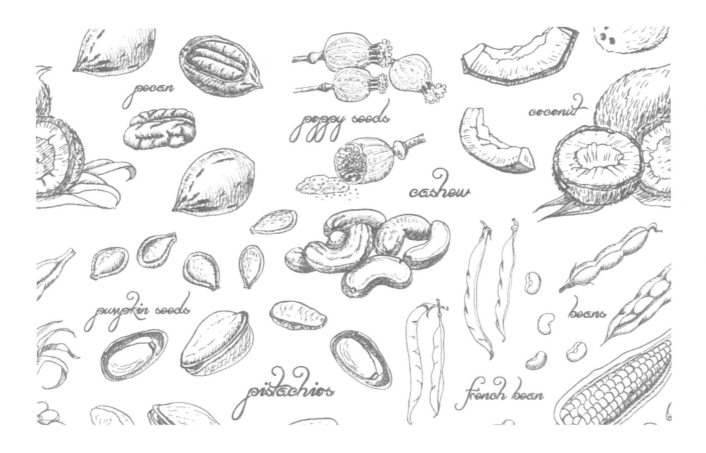

ABOUT THE AUTHOR

Steven Dowding is the owner of an organic farm near Mason City (Iowa). He cultivates his own garden, intending to safeguard heirloom seeds from extinction, ancient varieties of vegetables resistant to diseases and endowed with good nutritional properties. He has been a seed saver for almost 25 years now.

It was January 1996, and while it was raining outside, he was bored leafing through the catalogs of the seed companies that he had found one after the other. Determined to order seeds for spring, Steven found these catalogs very similar, with the same varieties of vegetables, tomatoes, carrots, peppers, zucchinis, and eggplants; the names changed, but the shapes and colors were always the same.

So, Steven decided to go to the countryside, looking for something different. He abandoned the city and his previous activity as a herbalist. He chose to live and work full-time as an organic farmer and seed saver, trying to implement a project for a family garden that would ensure him and his family good food self-sufficiency.

Steven is a vegetarian, and he makes sure to have on his table not only vegetables and fruits obtained without the use of pesticides but also the flavors, aromas, and fragrances that no longer inhabit modern farm products.

Steven is also a book writer; he constantly connects with seed saving networks across the United States, widening his searches by sending letters to look for seeds suitable for organic farming. As a pro seed saver, he is convinced that the plants he would obtain from sources produced with organic methods would be stronger and more resistant to disease.

Steven lives in Iowa with his family and his dog, Buck, who also helps him grow seeds!

TABLE OF CONTENTS

pumpkin seeds

poppy seeds

BOOK 3. SEED SAVING & STORING ADVANCED HACKS:
A Collection of No-Brainer Methods to Build Your Seed Bank, and Live the Frugal Gardening Style. Amish Tricks Included .p 56

BOOK 4. HEIRLOOM, HYBRID, ORGANIC & GMO SEEDS:
Understand the Differences between Various Types of Seeds and Build Your Seed Bank without Headaches. Includes Gardening Secrets to Never Buy Vegetables Again p. 80

BOOK 5. GARDEN GERMINATION TECHNIQUES:
A Climate-Proof Guide to Germinate Your Seeds 5 Times Faster and Scale Up Seed Saving in a Few Weeks p. 99

BOOK 6. SEED SAVING FOR PREPPERS | OFF-GRID SURVIVAL HACKS REVEALED:

How to Create Your Own Survival Seed Kit and Harvest, Store, and Preserve Seeds to Build a Time-Proof Long Term Pantry p. 125

BOOK 7. MAKE MONEY WITH YOUR BELOVED SEEDS:

Learn how to Sell Excess Seeds, Monetize Your Hard Work and Make Infinite ROI p. 148

CONCLUSION: IT'S UP TO YOU p. 160

INTRODUCTION

They are not heroes, yet they are doing their part to save the planet. Anonymous and silent, they are the custodians of diversity and traditions. They are called seed savers, and they are more and more, day after day.

Farmers or simple nature lovers, the seed savers are men and women who decide to safeguard and pass on to posterity a forgotten heritage that would otherwise be lost. Seed saving, in fact, is the activity of collecting and storing the seeds of endangered species, in order not to make them disappear.

This is not a particularly complicated activity: seed savers are primarily passionate and mindful people who privately cultivate varieties of flowering and fruit plants that are now archived and unknown to most. Why do they do it? Because they have at heart not only their own survival but also that of the entire planet. And of Nature in general.

Since 1990, the ancient species - that is the exact expression by which the varieties that are no longer cultivated are indicated - that have ended up forgotten and disappeared from the agri-food market are many: over 75% of the existing genetic diversity. 75 %! Not a tiny loss: far from it.

Without mentioning the connected, lost profits: the market for ancient species could, in fact, be worth around 11 billion American dollars. Thanks to the law of the market, which selects the highest demand as winning – and therefore as worthy of grabbing the supremacy of production – (and ruthlessly discards second and third choices), many agri-food products have gone lost. The disappearance of varieties of fruit, vegetables, and flowers - the so-called "genetic erosion" - is at its maximum.

A slight melancholy comes to think about it, but that's precisely how it is: the biological diversification of the past no longer exists. For example, there are almost 3,000 different types of apples, of which more than a hundred are of Italian origin. Yet, on the fruit and vegetable stalls, the varieties are always the same, and a few more than a dozen. Suffice it to say that 70% of Trentino's production is occupied by the Golden apple, which nonetheless has American origins. Or what remains of the varieties of watermelon: today, only one remains. And it is precisely here that seed savers come into play: thanks to their work of exchanging and preserving ancient seeds, despite the dominance of some specific products on the market, it is still possible to taste the rare species of the past. Rare delicacies, such as broccoli and persimmons.

The melancholy of knowing that we have gradually become thinner, reduced, and unified, instead of enriching our vocabulary, knowledge, and even our taste with thousands of different flavors and colors. To put it simply, we have lost the joy and uniqueness of diversity. But all is not lost.

Seed saving is an increasingly spreading activity supported by prominent personalities (including Vandana Shiva, a famous Indian activist who has been fighting GMOs and globalization for years) all over the world. There are many associations that support seed saving: from the Irish Seed Saver Association to the Canadian Seed of Diversity, which aims is to educate about the environment and ancient species, to bring them back to light and preserve their genetic heritage.

In fact, seeds are priceless and can be freely exchanged and donated. Being a seed saver means conserving and promoting biodiversity, saving hundreds of varieties from extinction. The effort is minimal, and the result is impressive. And incredibly tasty.

And the reason for this book is all here: recover the flavor of the past, reconnect to our present through the discovery of saving the seeds, and, ultimately, write a completely different future page from the promise - dark and standardized - of this moment.

And here's how we'll tackle the topic through the pages of the seven books waiting for you.

- **BOOK 1: Seed Saving History | The Journey Begins**: Go Back to Basics, Learn from the Past to Improve Your Future, and Be the Next Seed Master. In this book, you will learn how important it is to enter the world seed savers network for the environment and also for your legacy.

- **BOOK 2: Seed Saving & Storing for Beginners:** How to Harvest, Store and Keep Every Seed Fresh for Years, without Unpleasant Surprises. Seed Saving Demystified! The art of saving seeds will have no more secrets: all the techniques to start this new and exciting activity!

- **BOOK 3: Seed Saving & Storing Advanced Hacks:** A Collection of No-Brainer Methods to Build Your Seed Bank, and Live the Frugal Gardening Style. Amish Tricks Included. All the advanced methods and excellent tips you want to know to take your practice to the next level!

- **BOOK 4: Heirloom, Hybrid, Organic & GMO Seeds:** Understand the Differences between Various Types of Seeds and Build Your Seed Bank without Headaches. Includes Gardening Secrets to Never Buy Vegetables Again. Discover the difference between seed to seed and what it means to choose one variety over another. And how to build your own seed bank!

- **BOOK 5: Garden Germination Techniques:** A Climate-Proof Guide to Germinate Your Seeds 5 Times Faster and Scale Up Seed Saving in a Few Weeks. All methods - including the most advanced ones - for germinating your seeds without secrets.

- **BOOK 6: Seed Saving for Preppers** | Off Grid Survival Hacks Revealed: How to Create Your Own Survival Seed Kit and Harvest, Store and Preserve Seeds to Build a Time-Proof Long Term Pantry. Get ready to grow your seeds for the end of the world!

- **BOOK 7: Make Money with Your Beloved Seeds:** Learn how to Sell Excess Seeds, Monetize Your Hard Work and Make Infinite ROI. How this beneficial passion will become a successful business!

Are you ready to dig in?
Let's go!

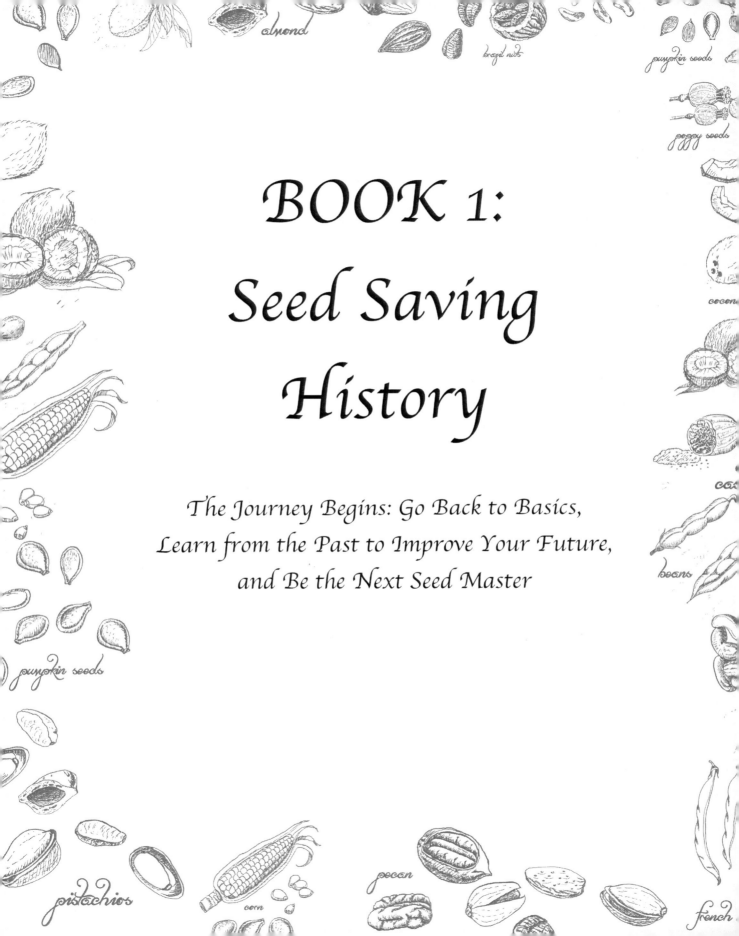

BOOK 1:
Seed Saving History

The Journey Begins: Go Back to Basics,
Learn from the Past to Improve Your Future,
and Be the Next Seed Master

Chapter 1.
THE HOUSE IS ON FIRE

Before deciding to write this book, I thought about it a lot, and it wasn't easy. If on the one hand, in fact, I felt the urgency to tell my dear people and the whole world how much beauty was being reborn from my hands and also thanks to my trust in Nature, on the other hand, I was pervaded by the diametrically opposite sensation.

We are at such an advanced level of loss of global wealth and biodiversity that I have asked myself several times: what is the point?

The house is on fire, quoting Greta Thunberg, governments don't reverse course to save the planet from global warming and we can't help it... but is it really like that? Do we really have nothing in hand?

And, making this reflection, I stopped and looked at myself through the mirror near a tomato plant, which I use to reflect sunlight: I had a handful of seeds in my hands.

In that instant, I cleared my mind of all doubts: I held power to help Nature, even by planting these few crucial seeds.

And so I planted them. Every day for the following five years, gathering satisfaction and a magnificent cultural, personal, and even global diversity.

Yes, because every act of ours is a national good, and we, too, in our small way, can contribute to making the Earth a better place. Because we belong to the Earth, we can take care of it.

Before explaining who seed savers are, who we are, and who you are about to become, let's try to know a little about the basics and the history of the recent past and how this noble activity was born: only in this way, will we learn from the past to improve our future. Only this way will you become the next seed master and embrace who you truly are.

Chapter 2.
UNPRECEDENTED LOSS

According to the Global Assessment Report by IPBES, the UN's Intergovernmental Platform on Biodiversity, human actions have altered nature, causing an 'unprecedented' global biodiversity loss.

The terrestrial and marine environments have been significantly modified, and about 1 million plant and animal species are at risk of extinction, something that has never occurred in the history of humanity. An alarming picture characterized by a series of threats to biological diversity introduced by the Anthropocene, the new current geological era in which human activities are changing the course of planetary evolution and influencing ecosystems and biodiversity.

Habitat destruction, soil and water pollution, the spread of invasive alien species, climate change, and over-exploitation of natural resources are among the main factors in biodiversity loss.

And losing biodiversity means losing a source of natural resources that are crucial for human needs and activities, losing decisive biological principles for the production of current and future medicines, and losing natural systems of protection from extreme events produced by climate change.

And it also means losing an infinite wealth of genetic material helpful in adapting to the new and significant changes produced by man, for a better understanding of life, and for defending ourselves against existing and future diseases.

Losing biodiversity also means losing the most precious ally against the harmful effects produced by man on the climate and the other so-called planetary boundaries.

The idea that there are limits or planetary boundaries that must not be exceeded, including the weight of human activities, to keep planet Earth as we have inherited it, has been around for some time.

In 2009, a group of Earth and Environmental Scientists identified nine planetary boundaries closely connected with nine environmental processes caused by man.

These boundaries consist of the following:

- climate change (concentration of carbon dioxide in the atmosphere);
- ocean acidification;
- biogeochemical nitrogen (N) and phosphorus (P) cycle;
- global use of freshwater;
- land use (land area converted to arable land);
- ozone depletion;
- chemical pollution;
- atmospheric aerosol load;
- loss of biological diversity (extinction rate).

Planetary boundaries define, so to speak, the edges of a safe space for humanity within which it is possible to continue to develop and thrive for future generations.

The boundaries mentioned above have already been crossed in as many as 4 of the nine processes considered. Globally, human activities related to agriculture and food contribute to the transgression of four of the nine planetary boundaries.

This means that in those specific areas, the pressure exerted by human action has long since exceeded the saturation threshold. Losing biodiversity also means increasing the planet's desertification; from the estimates provided, it seems that 12 million hectares of fertile land are desertified every year.

Desertification produced directly or indirectly by land use changes and deforestation that destroys natural habitats - such as tropical forests - is responsible for about half of emerging zoonoses, infectious diseases that can be transmitted from animals to humans.

The destruction of forests can expose humans to new forms of contact with microbes and the wild species that host them because millions of unknown species are believed to live in these ecosystems, including viruses, bacteria, fungi, and other parasites.

The development of zoonoses is also possible through the wildlife trade, the illegal killing of wild animals for food, and direct contact with animal parts.

Emerging zoonoses of wild origin could represent the greatest threat to the health of the world's population in the future.

The increasing human impact on ecosystems and wildlife, combined with that of global climate change, weakens natural ecosystems and facilitates the spread of pathogens, increasing human exposure to these risks.

In the last decade, therefore, the 'One Health' approach has increasingly established itself on a global level, which recognizes how human beings' health is closely linked to that of animals, plants, the environment, and ecosystems: a holistic health concept. Because only by recognizing that our health and well-being are closely linked to those of the nature that hosts us we can guarantee our species from the most harmful effects of pandemics.

Therefore, a new global agreement between people and nature is desirable, which must provide for halving our footprint on nature, arresting the loss of natural habitats, and halting the extinction of living species.

Of the nine 'alarm' areas of the current state of health of the planet and, consequently, of man, what concerns us most closely is precisely the last one, which is the continuous erosion of biodiversity. Why is biodiversity so important, especially in our discourse linked to saving seeds?

We will find the answer in the next Chapter.

Chapter 3.
WHY IS BIODIVERSITY CRUCIAL?

Biodiversity enhances the productivity of any ecosystem (agricultural land, a forest, a lake, and so on). In fact, it has been shown that biodiversity loss contributes to energy and food insecurity, increases susceptibility to Natural disasters, such as tropical storms or floods, decreases the grade of health within society, reduces access to water resources, and threatens cultural traditions.

Each species, whether small or large, plays a specific role in the ecosystem in which it lives, and precisely under its function, it helps the ecosystem to maintain its vital balance. Even a species that is not endangered on a global scale can play an essential role locally. Its decrease at this scale will have an impact on the stability of the habitat. For example, a greater variety of species means a greater variety of crops, a greater diversity of species ensures the natural sustainability of all life forms, and a healthy ecosystem better tolerates a disturbance, disease, or bad weather and reacts better.

Biodiversity, in addition to its value per se, is also essential because it is a source of goods, resources, and services for man: the so-called ecosystem services. All human, animal, and plant communities on the planet directly or indirectly benefit from these services, which specialists classify as support, supply, regulation, and cultural services.

The same services are vital in building the economy of human communities and states. For example, plant biodiversity, both in cultivated and wild plants, forms the basis of agriculture, enabling the production of food and contributing to the health and nutrition of the entire world population.

Over a third of human food - from fruits to seeds to vegetables - would fail if there were no pollinators (bees, wasps, butterflies, flies, but also birds and bats), which, visiting flowers, carry pollen from the anthers male on the stigma of the female organ, resulting in fertilization.

There are 130,000 plants to which bees are essential for pollination. Unfortunately, bees have been undergoing a dramatic decline in recent years due to the destruction and degradation of habitats, some diseases, pesticide treatments, and herbicides in agriculture. Some ongoing research also hypothesizes the influence of electromagnetic waves, which are increasing due to mobile phone towers. It seems that the radiation interferes with the orientation system of the insects, preventing them from tracing the way to the hive and leading them to scatter and die elsewhere.

In the past, genetic resources have allowed the improvement of cultivated and bred species and will continue to perform this function in the future. This variability will also make it possible to obtain new plant varieties to cultivate or animals to raise and to adapt to changing climatic and environmental conditions.

Biodiversity supplies nourishment (vegetables and animals), fibers for fabrics (cotton, wool, etc.), and raw materials for the production of energy (wood and fossil minerals) and is the basis for medicines.

The loss and impoverishment of biodiversity have heavy impacts on the economy and society, reducing the availability of food, energy, and medicinal resources. Currently, the world drug market is worth 650 billion dollars, and almost half is based on drugs taken, directly or indirectly, from the plant and animal kingdoms.

To summarize: Nature's greatest strength is biodiversity, the vast number of different plants and animals.

The intensive use of resources, however, makes us concentrate on a few varieties (of cereals, vegetables, etc.): the first 30, today, supply 95% of the world's food. In 1903, for example, 578 types of beans were grown in the USA; today, only 32. The death of one of these plants can have severe consequences.

For this reason, preserving even the ancient seeds that are no longer used is essential, taking care to keep the new ones safe.

This is how our ancestors arrived at this conclusion that is fundamental to the history and survival of our beloved planet.

Chapter 4.
IN THE HEART OF THE ARCTIC

Imagine landing in Longyearbyen, in the Norwegian archipelago of Svalbard, beyond the Arctic Circle. It is the northernmost one in the world among the civil airports with regular activity.

When you step off the plane, you are immediately smacked by the freezing air. Then you take a small road that climbs up the side of the mountain and, after about three kilometers, ends up in a square lay-by. There is nothing there except a door carved into a triangular structure that looks like a sliver of glass and concrete thrown against the mountain. Above the door, you can see the grates of a powerful ventilation system. And above that, an artistic installation that recalls the ice, the cold, and the Arctic.

Where did you go? An inscription near the door helps you: Svalbard Global Seed Vault, the global seed bank active since 2008.

Longyearbyen is a town on the island of Spitzbergen in the Svalbard archipelago (halfway between Norway and the North Pole, in the round). Isolated, cold, and far from strategic points that could involve it in the event of war, it is the ideal place for the Svalbard Global Seed Vault, the business that preserves our most precious assets: seeds.

Inside, after a tunnel that goes into the mountain for a hundred meters, three large warehouses have been dug to store specimens of all, absolutely all, the plant species in the world. And not only those that are grown today: even seeds of plants that are no longer found in Nature. Inside the halls, there are 18 degrees below zero, kept constant by a refined cooling system. And, even in the event of a failure, the temperature would never rise above zero because the ground there is permafrost, i.e., a surface that remains frozen even in summer.

Why is this place so important? As we just saw earlier, life on our planet depends on biodiversity: if we cultivated only one type of plant in the world and it developed a disease, our existence would be at risk. Seed banks like this one ensure that there is always a chance to recover a lost species or to find new crops resistant to threats. In short, these places contain invaluable wealth... Other than the 'useless' banknotes!

Here is what you can find inside this peculiar bank:

The bank: Today, only the central hall is almost complete. Exploiting them all, there is room for 4.5 million different varieties;

The tunnel: In this tunnel, 100 meters long, the natural temperature varies between -3 and -5°C;

The rooms are about 10 m wide, 27 m long, and 6 m high. The doors are locked, and there is always control staff;

Control room, to keep an eye on the temperature and other parameters;

Refrigeration: A system maintains the temperature at -18 °C;

Security: Two airtight chambers and a multi-lock door secure the site;

Storage and Warehouses: Seeds are stored in bags and boxes on shelves. A computerized code system allows you to find them.

The Svalbard Global SeedVault is one of the most known leading seed banks in the world and was inaugurated in February 2008 in the presence of numerous world authorities, including the Nobel Peace Prize winner Wangari Maathai.

An actual germplasm bank, a bulwark against the risk of losing plant genetic heritage.

Chapter 5.
THE INESTIMABLE VALUE OF SEED BANKS

S valbard is not the only seed bank in the world, but it is the safest and therefore is also used by others as an emergency deposit. For example, the desert climate seed collection was in Aleppo, Syria, but was destroyed following the war. Fortunately, a duplicate of those specimens is preserved on Svalbard, from which other seeds have been grown. So far, it has been the only case using this structure's seeds.

There are also over a thousand seed banks in the world, also called 'germplasm banks.' Each of these decides which seeds to give preference to, wildflowers, native vegetables, and cereals of species native to different regions of the planet.

Other institutes have a global mission to select and preserve varieties of grains with particular natural characteristics and not be determined in the laboratory by man.

The Global Crop Diversity Trust, for example, focuses its attention exclusively on a selection of priority crops at a global level, such as apples, barley, oats, peas, potatoes, rice, beans, etc. This body carries out its activity following the directives indicated in a treaty, The International

Treaty on PlantGeneticResources for Food and Agriculture (PGRFA), signed by over thirty countries. The Treaty created a global system to provide farmers, scholars, and anyone in need with access to the genetic heritage of certain plants. In this case, access to the seeds is allowed on the condition that the results of the studies undertaken can benefit all. Even poisonous plants can have a collective utility, despite their uninviting characteristics.

It might seem strange, but the seed bank was born as a network for exchanging and protecting seeds. A place where seeds are collected, born, grown, to be selected, and distributed according to a free and continuous cycle.

Also called seed libraries, seed banks in agriculture allow you to borrow seeds, as happens with an ordinary book, and then return them as soon as you have managed to multiply them.

The exchange of seeds, the recovery of sowing calendars, and news on the use of sources try to spread, even via the web, the most ancient agricultural practices to amplify and disseminate sustainable cultivation methods, agriculture capable of coexisting with Nature.

On the other hand, the most recent projects are of utmost importance.

One is called Future Seeds and is at least as iconic as its Norwegian twin, the Global Seed Vault of the Svalbard Islands.

The new world plant genome bank in Palmira, Colombia, costing 17 million dollars, designed to be completely sustainable and just inaugurated, hosts mainly seeds and germplasms from that part of the world, tropical, with a particular concentration of cassava varieties, of which it contains samples of over 6,100 types, forage grasses (22,600) and beans (just under 38,000).

Furthermore, Future Seeds was designed to allow and indeed stimulate international collaborations through meetings, seminars, partnerships, and public access, including the school one, to raise awareness of the importance of plant biodiversity in the younger generations.

The bank officially started its activity at a time when the war in Ukraine is, among other things, reminding the whole world how precious seeds are and how essential their custody is.

Seed banks host millions of plant varieties and species, many of which are yet to be studied, often endowed with characteristics of resistance that could represent salvation for humanity in the coming years.

Places like these host – it is estimated – over seven million plant varieties and species, many of which are still to be studied and often equipped with characteristics of resistance to unfavorable environmental conditions or parasites and diseases that could represent salvation for humanity over the next few years.

And this is exactly the reason why the first seed savers in history were born.

Chapter 6.
SEED SELECTION AND STORAGE: A HISTORY

They were agronomists, botanists, explorers, geneticists, and philosophers. The most potent names include Mendel, Jean-Jacques Rousseau, Darwin, George Washington, and also Vavilov. This last name will say little or nothing to many, like me up until recently.

Nikolaj Ivanovich Vavilov, with a primary role in world agriculture, is a Russian agronomist of the early twentieth century. We owe him the particular attention that he was among the first to dedicate to plant genetics, a science born recently. He put it into practice to select new wheat varieties, with the romantic idea of discovering particularly resistant ones capable of helping the Russian people gripped by hunger during and after years of brutal wars.

If you read the story of this character, you will be fascinated. In 1887, Vavilov was born in Moscow, and here, in 1906, he enrolled at the agricultural institute. In 1911 he graduated and immediately began traveling the world for study purposes.

During this period, he met one of the founders of genetics, W. Bateson. He also deepens the study of the experiences made by Nazareno Strampelli, an Italian geneticist and agronomist.

In a period of great suffering and transformation in Russia, Vavilov was entrusted with the direction of the pan-Soviet Lenin Academy of Agricultural Sciences. In the ten years following 1920, after more than sixty trips around the world, he manages to put together an extraordinary collection of seeds between wheat and wild plants. The extensive seed collection is kept in St. Petersburg.

In 1934 Vavilov had already opened over 400 research centers and experimental stations throughout the country, where 20,000 researchers and technicians worked, and had thus led the Soviet Union to the top of the world in botanical research and its applications. In the meantime, his institute had become the VIR, the Vavilov Institute of All Russia for industrial plants, today for plant genetics (it should be noted that, in the name change, which took place a few years ago, the remaining part is that relating to all Russia): the first seed bank in the world, which is 1940 already housed over 200,000 samples (today there are 325,000).

With the death of Lenin, his supporter, and the advent of Stalin, the fortunes of Vavilov come to an end, and the problems begin. Vavilov had continued to travel to every corner of the planet for a total of 115 missions in 64 countries, all aimed at studying the plants of the most diverse latitudes and creating cultural and scientific exchanges. But shortly after, following the famine caused by Stalin's senseless agricultural policies, Trofim Lysenko was preferred over him, hostile to any hypothesis of Mendelian genetics and supporter of the so-called vernalization, an utterly unsubstantiated theory according to which, to contrast the insufficiency of the crops, it was necessary to extend the crops to the northernmost and coldest areas of Russia, also resorting to expedients which, if they had not indirectly caused millions of deaths, would today seem grotesque. Vernalization had conquered Stalin, who in 1941 condemned Vavilov to capital punishment, then commuted to twenty years of prison so harshly that death occurred from starvation in 1943. His last mission, a few weeks before his arrest in the summer of 1940, was in already fatal lands: Ukraine and Belarus.

However, his ideas had made schools and proselytes. During the siege of the Germans on the city of St. Petersburg, his collaborators managed to preserve the texts of his studies and the large collection he had created.

His scholars, in fact saved the VIR only to then risk being looted or completely destroyed during the Nazi siege of Leningrad, which began in September 1941 and lasted 28 months until January 1944.

The story of Russian men who managed to save dozens of thousands of seeds, partly resisting inside the institute even the very rigid temperatures of the winter of 1941-42, which reached - 30°C and beyond, partly carrying tens of thousands of samples to a secret deposit in the Ural mountains, fleeing with the buds hidden in her clothes, she became a legend. During the three winters of the siege, dozens of researchers holed up in the VIR building. They protected the seeds by sacrificing every available watt to maintain environmental conditions compatible with the accessions' survival, resisting the enemy's attacks and then those of the rats, often at the cost of their lives (the victims of starvation can be counted in the dozens). But in the end, thanks to the reproduction of 6,000 seeds made at the Pavlovsk station, 45 km from the center, they saved thousands of plants that still represent an invaluable heritage.

Some of these preferred to starve to death rather than consume the jealously preserved seeds.

A behavior that only a true seed grower can fully understand.

A love for this profession which, at times, is even worth more than the life of us poor single individuals. As we have seen, on the other hand, the fate of entire humanity is at stake.

The VIR is the model that inspired all the subsequent banks, each specialized in part in local vegetation of which, in addition to the seeds, tissues and grafts are preserved to allow the study of the plants and also to save them in the event of natural catastrophes or wars. Just as happened in Syria, with the saving of ICARDA seeds.

The story is very similar to that of the VIR but concerns a contemporary war: the Syrian one. Also, in that case, there was fear of losing the yellow gold of the Middle East, i.e., the thousands of seeds and accessions kept in Tel Hadia, 20 km from Aleppo, at the International Center for Agricultural Research in the Dry Areas, better known as ICARDA. The story of that equally fortunate rescue of 116,000 accessions was told, among others, by one of the protagonists, Mariana Yazbek, in Nature Plants, as well as in a report from the New Yorker, and demonstrates what it still means today to be able to count on a germplasm biobank.

In 2008, ICARDA researchers were among the first to send their seeds to Svalbard, asking Norwegian researchers to duplicate at least part of them. Between 2012 and 2014, with the worsening of the area, they made new sendings, which continued until the institute's closure due to the war, which sadly became indispensable in 2015. But at that time, fortunately, the Global Seed Vault accounted for 83% of Syrian samples. And the Norwegians had worked on those seeds, as had dozens of ICARDA researchers who fled to different countries.

All this made it possible, in that same year, with the war not yet over, to plant thousands of seeds in the experimental fields of the universities and research centers of Morocco and Lebanon, i.e., to save a large part of them.

In 2020, there were 43 countries hosting plants arriving from Tel Hadia, and over the past five years, Syrian accessions have given birth to more than 100,000 new plants, resulting in 81,000 new samples shipped back to Svalbard, together with plant accessions Moroccan and Lebanese and other Mediterranean and Middle Eastern countries, all very resistant to arid climates. Meanwhile, ICARDA staff has scattered 98% of its seeds and accessions in 11 different international biobanks.

Today, as already mentioned above, there are several international banks in the world and over 1,700 public biobanks of this type, including the Asian Center for Vegetable Research and Development in Taiwan, known for its extraordinary deposit of eggplants and the like, the International Corn Improvement Center and Wheat Institute of Mexico City, the International Crop Research Institute for the Semi-Arid Tropics in India and the International Rice Research Institute of the Philippines, as well as an unknown number of private banks, where companies study the new varieties away from prying eyes for commercial purposes.

At the same time, an attempt is being made to standardize the language, taking into account contemporary evolutions of taxonomy, because it was realized that there were very many overlaps, depending on the denominations given to the same plant in the various countries, and that the filing systems were not the same everywhere, and this gave rise to many errors of evaluation.

It was the same for peppers: thanks to international collaboration, they have homogeneously described several accessions that once would have been unthinkable to study.

Finally, studying thousands of samples from all over the world, in addition to possible commercial applications in non-food fields (for example, pharmaceuticals), can have unforeseen consequences.

The data from so many accessions have allowed researchers to genetically reconstruct the evolution of a plant that has probably been consumed for less than 5,000 years, whose main varieties, sweet and spicy, have taken two completely different paths. Both originally from South America, they passed through Africa, through the first trades and then the slave routes. From there, sweet peppers spread throughout the Mediterranean basin, Europe, the Balkans, and the Near East, while hot peppers, circumnavigating the African continent, especially with Portuguese navigators and traders, arrived in Asia and, across the Pacific Ocean, back to the American continent. In both cases, they have profoundly influenced the eating habits and, with them, the culture and economic development of the different populations, similar to what happened with the tomato, introduced above all by the Spaniards on similar routes.

All of this has a new importance today because identifying the areas where a plant has spread helps concentrate efforts in specific directions and enriches our knowledge of history.

Chapter 7.
SEED SAVERS AND FOOD SOVEREIGNTY

We often forget it, but we all have special rights concerning food: it is the so-called 'food sovereignty' which implies the development of a system based on bio-cultural diversity at the local level, a system which, moreover, requires knowledge, techniques, and technologies radically different from those imposed in recent decades by the scientific and industrial apparatus.

In this regard, we recall that the seed is the first and crucial link in the food chain. All the crops that feed us come from seeds selected and handed down by farmers from all over the world, from generation to generation, creating that dynamic bio-diversity that makes plants capable of adapting to the variability of soils, climates, agricultural practices, and human needs.

The industrialization of agriculture, on the other hand, is a recent phenomenon, nonetheless capable of revolutionizing the rural equilibrium that has now been consolidated for centuries: peasant seeds suffer the threat of cannibalization by seeds 'improved' in the laboratory, GMOs (Genetic Modified Organisms), to be more resistant to pesticides and fertilizers.

According to the FAO, this massive industrialization has already eroded 75% of biodiversity but has also led to severe environmental and health damage. The hiatus is evident: on the one hand, there is the dominance of the multinationals on the market in which, at best, farmers are left with the choice of either conforming or, on the contrary, being reduced to occupying marginal niches; on the other, there is the model of 'social' agriculture with the rights of those who work and those who consume the food at the center.

The battle against GMOs, therefore, is, above all, a battle for the sovereignty of people to ensure that they can choose their own model of production, distribution, and consumption of food, refusing the spread of a model based on exploitation, now presented as inevitable and essential. For peasant movements, the opposition to globalization and, therefore, to GMOs is a struggle against a standard model that usurps them from the right/duty to be able to choose what and how to produce.

In the face of food and environmental challenges that are becoming increasingly urgent, therefore, the ability to adapt crops to the amplification of climate change and the decrease in energy and chemical inputs requires bringing farmers' rights back to the center, giving them back the right to choose, exchange, select and multiply seeds locally.

That 'invisibility' has now been broken by the multiplied mobilizations in every corner of the planet, turning the spotlight on these new foods and making public opinion aware, critical and involved. GMOs have had the 'merit' of reawakening the attention of the general Western public to food, how and by whom it is grown, processed, and marketed, as well as reopening the debate on the role of research, science evolution 21st-century society, even within the same scientific world. On the other hand, the subject's political repercussions also involved seed savers.

Rather than supporting and deregulating the use of new genetic engineering techniques, which pose high risks to health and the environment and therefore need to be regulated by the GMO directive, the sector needs change based on agrobiodiversity and a wide range of open-pollinated varieties to lay the foundations for sustainable food production.

The scope of the legislation should limit the marketing of seeds to commercial activities aimed at professional users. The current legislation harms the hobbyist sector, which has different incentives, motivations, and risks compared to commercial operators. The sale of amateur varieties should not be regulated so that they can play a crucial role in preserving diversity.

Seed conservation networks are formal or informal entities that trade and market varieties in limited quantities on a non-profit basis to conserve diversity. These networks are essential, and their work should not be restricted but outside the legislation's scope.

There should be no mandatory registration for these networks and individual actors. There shouldn't be an excessive expense to register seeds, let alone excessive speculation of the activities of seed savers, but absolute protection of these activities.

Safeguarding seed savers means safeguarding ourselves, Nature, and the entire Universe. And I'm not exaggerating.

Chapter 8.
SEED SAVING: THE JOURNEY BEGINS

We *must take back the right to conserve seeds and biodiversity. The right to nutrition and healthy food. The right to protect the earth and its species.*

So says Dr. Vandana Shiva, scientist, environmentalist, writer, and philosopher, counted among the theorists of social ecology, a current of thought that combines social and political-ecological themes.

According to this theory, the world requires a paradigm shift in the use of our planet's resources, which would be capable of feeding everyone if we respected Nature and equality between men were effective.

Food democracy is at the heart of the agenda for democracy and human rights, at the heart of the agenda for ecological sustainability and social justice. The question is not how much rich nations can give: the question is how much less they can take.

Man and Nature have lived in harmony since ancient times, respecting each other's measures.

Starting from the Industrial Revolution, then, with the use of coal and the exploitation of fossil resources and, later, after the Second World War, with the so-called 'Green Revolution,' the man-nature balance has drastically changed, to the greater detriment of natural resources and the climate situation.

The absurdity is this: regardless of what Governments and States have done (very little) or decide to do for the environment in the future, we can ask ourselves one question, and it is urgent: what can we do?

In the meantime, in the wake of the example of Navdanya, movements of collectors of seed, the so-called seed savers, have begun to emerge worldwide at all latitudes.

Seed savers are people who, both for peasant culture and for the desire to save and pass on the traditions of their territory to their children, preserving for them unapproved flavors such as those of intensive production, undertake to search for untreated ancient seeds to conserve and reproduce them through strictly biological systems.

Not only are the global movements remarkable, but it is also ordinary people who are more attentive to ecology and want to feed themselves ethically and sustainably; therefore, they are increasingly trying to buy organic products with proven origin.

But that's not all: in recent years, many seed exchange associations have been founded, and some also organize courses to become seed savers. These courses teach how to search for seeds in the area and hand down the techniques for reproduction and conservation.

Many young people, often from different work experiences, are realizing the potential of organic and sustainable agricultural production and are engaging in the recovery and use of seeds and ancient cultivation systems to guarantee organic quality and 'high nutritional value.

Even if timidly, we can say that on the horizon, we can glimpse that paradigm shift so much desired by those who, like Dr. Shiva and the seed savers, believe that the right to biodiversity, the conservation of seeds, and organic and sustainable agriculture for the Nature are synonymous with democracy.

We have the right to preserve what belongs to us, but we have the sacred duty to care for the environment, even starting from a pile of seeds.

Are you ready to become the next seed master and to be a part of this remarkable movement of silent but precious modern heroes?

BOOK 2:
Seed Saving
& Storing for
Beginners:

How to Harvest, Store and Keep Every Seed
Fresh for Years, without Unpleasant Surprises.
Seed Saving Demystified!

Chapter 1.
SEED SAVING DEMYSTIFIED

Learning how to obtain and store the seeds of your favorite vegetables is important if you want to transform your vegetable garden or terrace cultivation into something more than a hobby.

Not only ornamental plants but also fruit and vegetables suitable for your family's consumption or, why not, for sale.

In this book, I will explain how to start collecting and storing the seeds so they are ready to be replanted the following year. I bet it will be much easier for you to grow your favorite crops without necessarily having to go to a specialized professional every year.

In the past, saving seeds for the next planting or the following year was a common practice. The farmers, following the rhythm of the seasons, were very attentive to this work and often exchanged ideas and advice, as well as the seeds themselves. That system guaranteed the survival of the gardens and the balance of life within the community in the short and long term.

Today, unfortunately, this system has been lost, and the activity of collecting and storing seeds has become frightening (we learned about it in Book 1), especially for the planet's sake. Very few locally adapted varieties are available today: varieties that have particular characteristics, so valuable for the 'clean' grower, of flavor and resistance to adversity. Also, very few horticulturists today do what came naturally to their ancestors, save the seeds of their crops. The diversity of life (biodiversity), essential to our survival, is quietly eroding.

Until recently, all farmers were the plant heritage workers who supported us. Over the centuries, the collection of seeds made it possible to 'tame' wild plants, allowing communities to establish themselves.

Through years of conscious selection of fruits, vegetables, cereals, and flowers, the past farmers have produced the diversity of crops that we enjoy today.

Luckily, there are seed savers, both individuals and networks of associations, that deal with saving - literally - the seeds and contributing to their harvest and conservation for the following seasons. Precisely the content I want to convey to you in this Book 2.

Moreover, to save good seeds, you must follow what plants do naturally. But you have to start from a seed stock that is original and viable.

Today's mass production and distribution regulate plant cultivation and seed production globally. It is obvious to anyone that when plants are 'designed' for specific commercial purposes, other valuable characteristics are inevitably lost. Tomatoes harvested by machine, unloaded on conveyor belts, and shipped by truck long distances, must be challenging but not necessarily tasty or nutritious.

The result of these trends is that growers depend on hybrid vegetable and flower seeds controlled by large companies, which have to be repurchased annually at an additional cost to the growers.

Furthermore, hybrid plants are genetically uniform. Hybrid seeds produce virtually identical plants, which will all die together when there is a disease or insect pest problem. In a small vegetable garden, the differences between the plants allow for different reactions to pests. Uniformity is entirely contrary to the needs of the family garden.

All being considered, Seed Savers rose precisely to preserve the rich diversity of crops before they disappeared, both for our future and our descendants.

The Seed Savers is a network of people spread worldwide determined to recover free, non-patented seeds from the earth, plant them in their greenery, cultivate them and recover the regenerated seeds.

Seed Savers is used to preserving successive generations of rare seeds by donating or exchanging them to increase the diffusion of plants otherwise doomed to extinction. The importance of the natural heritage to be handed down to the future has inspired jewels that guard and contain those seeds and ornaments to wear whose value is determined by the preciousness of life inside them. Four transparent caskets enclose the treasure of biodiversity in the heart of clay, a treasure that we cannot possess except by returning it to the earth by taking care of it.

We can make ourselves independent again by collecting seeds and passing on knowledge about the propagation and use of plants. By regaining control of our seeds and food, we strengthen our security, the genetic integrity of our traditional crops, and the potential to develop valuable varieties adapted to the region's climate, soil, and local insects and diseases.

In practice, we can regain possession of our intuitive, unique relationship based on the knowledge of our territory with the land we tread and love. This enhances our curiosity about the cycles of living beings.

I hope this book will give you the confidence and the knowledge you need to become a true seed saver while protecting plant diversity.

The techniques are elementary to master: I will help you see at a glance whether the plant you have selected for seed harvesting suits your experience. As a beginner, for example, you can start with tomatoes, salads, and beans, as cross-pollination is impossible. This optimizes the chances of future seed purity.

You may initially decide to stick with just one variety, having obtained your endowment from a horticultural friend, a family seed company, the Seed Savers Network, your local horticulture club, or a permaculture group. Soon you'll have plenty of seeds and enough experience to continue to more challenging tasks.

Good job!

Before starting, I think you will be pleased to read this identikit of the seed saver, in which I am sure you will find yourself 101%!

This book is for you if…

… you are interested in agriculture and cultivation;

… you are interested in how seeds are studied, cultivated, and stored;

… you are curious about today's seeds but also about those that have disappeared from circulation;

… you are open to collaborating if discovering a new seed or new cultivation;

… you have a vision beyond 'your own garden,' aimed at safeguarding the environment;

… have the interests of the planet, biodiversity, and the green world at heart;

… you care about saving seeds from extinction, as you know the essential value of diversity for the balance of all living beings;

… you know the contribution that every single person can make in saving the environment;

… can't wait to start the noble art of saving seeds.

At this point, having cleared the field on what it means to embrace the seed saver lifestyle, we are ready… let's find out the path to walk to get you closer to becoming a seed master step by step!

Chapter 2.
SEEDS: WHAT TO KNOW

We have said that storing seeds is essential to restarting your favorite crops. But what is a seed? It is nothing but an egg transformed by the fertilization process. In short, the seed is the principal organ helpful for disseminating plants. The seeds are also poor in water, which is why they can boast a long shelf life.

The seed is the main reproductive organ of most higher terrestrial and aquatic plants. Its role as a species preserver is fundamental, as it can withstand very extreme external conditions without dying and even germinating later. Seeds are essential for plant dispersal, forest regeneration, and, in general, for the ecological succession of any ecosystem.

In nature, the seed serves as food for many species of animals. We can say that the seed is something fundamental for human beings, too, if we speak in agricultural terms, since without the seeds, we could not cultivate anything, and agriculture would not exist. What's more, the leading food of human beings consists directly or indirectly of seeds.

On the other hand, the seeds are used to manage wild populations in forests and to carry out reforestation; they also serve to conserve specific endangered species by preserving the plant germplasm because they can be kept alive for long periods. This helps us to maintain the most precious plant species and varieties for humans or for some ecosystems.

Thanks to the fact that science has been studying seeds for a long time, it is possible to have an excellent knowledge of the biology of many plants. To learn more about the conservation of certain species of flora and vegetation, the physiological characteristics of seeds, the mechanisms of dormancy and germination, the environmental conditions they need, their longevity, and their different uses for plant propagation and conservation of some plants.

<u>What Is the Origin of a Seed?</u>

We know that the seed is the primary reproductive unit of plants. Furthermore, it is complex since it is formed from the plant's ovule after fertilization and has complex survival mechanisms. Seeds are found in both angiosperms and gymnosperms. Although gymnosperms do not have actual flowers, the structure of the seeds of these plants is very similar to those that do have flowers.

The size of the seeds of different plant species can vary greatly. There are seeds of multiple sizes and shapes despite being an organ with a common origin to all species and performing the same function.

In terms of weight, there are tiny seeds, such as those of orchids weighing 0.1 mg, and others enormous such as those of the double Pacific coconut weighing 10 kg. Within the same plant community, the differences between dimensions are generally minor. However, they can vary up to six orders of magnitude.

To produce seeds, plants require a large amount of energy, so depending on the state of the plant, it can have a greater or lesser number of seeds, and these will be more or less large. Plants that produce smaller seeds can spread more widely and have a better chance of finding a place with more favorable environmental conditions to germinate and grow. However, such tiny seeds do not help in their growth, so the new seedling will have to draw on the resources that surround it as soon as possible. This carries a reasonably high risk of dying compared to those larger seeds. They also have less resistance to the defoliation effects of herbivores and are easily crushed by falling leaf litter. While the large numbers somewhat offset this, only a small fraction survive these crashes.

All being considered, you will be able to know something more about the seeds and the importance they have.

Moreover, as you are here to master your seed saving art, you should know that the seeds you will collect and store must have particular characteristics. They must therefore be:

- obtained with free pollination;
- ripe;
- healthy:

- with good color;
- without roughness.

Logically, there is no general guideline to carry out these characteristics systematically, as each seed follows a different collection, germination, and storage regime.

Generally speaking, however, a seed can be divided into three parts: the embryo, the nutritive tissue or parenchyma, and the integuments, which surround and protect the whole. The act of plant reproduction is called fertilization and occurs through pollination.

Inside the seed, the new plant is represented by the embryo, a seedling containing the sketches of the root system, the vegetative apex, and one or two embryonic leaves, called cotyledons. The endosperm is a trophic tissue in which the nutrients necessary to accumulate reserves are accumulated.

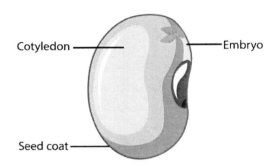

When ripe, the seed enters a phase of inactivity or dormancy, during which all vital functions are suspended to be restored when the conditions favorable for germination occur. The maintenance of potential viability is called 'germinability.' Some species can maintain germinability even for several years, others only for a short time, on the order of a few weeks. The duration of germinability also varies from seed to seed within the same species. Still, in general, a consistent number of seeds lose their ability to germinate after one-two year in most species: the biological meaning of seed dormancy is to overcome the critical environmental conditions so that the seed maintains germinability until the arrival of conditions favorable to the development of the seedling.

Environmental and endogenous factors of a hormonal nature regulate the duration of dormancy. The latter is based on biochemical mechanisms that are activated as a response to environmental stimuli to ensure that the germination process takes place in favorable conditions or that the preservation of the species is maintained when unfavorable events cause a decimation. For example, the seeds of species native to temperate zones can germinate only after going through a cold period, so germination can occur after the winter season has passed.

Once the awakening mechanisms are activated, germination begins with the imbibition phase: the seed absorbs water in order to bring the water content in the cells to levels compatible with the development of physiological processes.

In this phase, the seed increases in volume, while the protective integuments undergo a breakdown or breakage in the points of least resistance. With rehydration, cellular metabolism is activated, and the translocation of nutrients from the endosperm or cotyledons towards the embryonic axis and the start of growth activity manifest itself with the exit of the seedling from the integuments.

The actual germination ends with emergence, a phase in which the plant, drawing on residual reserves, acquires the ability to photosynthesize. The duration of the entire phase depends not only on factors intrinsic to the species but also on environmental factors and, in particular, on the temperature and humidity conditions.

Before delving into the basic essential methods for becoming a seed saver, here is a summary of what the 'seed saving' process means and include:

Seed Collection and Harvesting

The seeds should be harvested only from the healthiest and strongest plants. Therefore, the first step to ensure quality seeds for the following year is to select the best plants in the garden: robust and healthy seedlings that bear many fruits. Once you have identified the best plants, remember to wait for the right time to collect the seeds.

The best moment to harvest seeds depends on the variety of plants. Plant seeds, such as pumpkins, tomatoes, and melons, should be harvested when fully mature. Pease and beans, however, should be left on the plant until they are completely dry.

Seed Drying

Beans, okra, basil, peppers, and onions are all considered dry seeds. We should perform dry seed cleaning after the plant has completely dehydrated. If rain is a concern, you can harvest the shells and pods and place them in a dry, moisture-free area to continue the drying process.

You can start cleaning the seeds when the husk or pod crumbles easily in your hand. Remove the larger pieces and place the rest of the dough in a bowl. By shaking the bowl, the heavy pieces will rise to the top. To remove just the seeds, use a screen or mesh with just enough holes to allow the seeds to pass through. Repeat this process until only seeds remain.

Wet Seed Cleaning

Wet seeds include eggplants, wide squash varieties, and tomatoes. The cleaning process of wet seeds is much easier than its dry counterparts. One must be sure that the vegetable is fully ripe before harvesting. Once fully ripe, remove the vegetable from the stem, scoop out the pulp and seeds and mix them in a large bowl with water. The good seeds will sink, while the dead ones will rise to the surface with the pulp.

After removing the seeds, they must be dried before placing them in storage. Drain the excess water with a filter and dry the seeds with a paper towel. Spread the seeds on a plate and store them in a dry and cool place for a few days.

Seed Storage

Envelopes are an excellent way to store seeds as they can be easily labeled. Glass jars are also good for larger groupings.

Remember to label the seeds with the type and variety, where the original seed was purchased, and when it was harvested.

It is optimum to collect the seeds in a cool, dry place. Avoid environments that contain moisture, as this can encourage seeds to germinate or develop mold. Some seeds, such as potatoes and onions, can be stored in open containers.

Seed Longevity

Seeds can last from two to 10 years, depending on the type of seed and storage conditions. You can verify that your seeds are still good for planting by doing a germination test. If the seeds germinate successfully, then they are ready for another growing season.

Germination

Germination is the procedure by which an organism grows from a seed or spore.

This represents an essential step since it is a necessary test to verify if the previous steps of semen collection and storage have gone the right way.

Pro Tips

Avoid using hybrid seeds for next year's crop, as this could produce a completely different plant next season. Some plants are biennial, which means they don't produce seeds until their second year. We will address this topic in Book 4.

Chapter 3.
SEED SAVING: HARVESTING AND COLLECTING

With the arrival of cold weather, plants and vegetables begin to lose vigor and turn yellow and then leave the ground for the varieties that will be born the following year. For this reason, autumn and winter are the right seasons to select and collect the seeds that will give life to future plants.

So, how to proceed with the collection and then the conservation of the seeds? These are reasonably simple operations to perform but require some special attention.

For a good harvest, it is necessary to observe the characteristics of the plants from which you intend to take the seeds: the best species from which to obtain excellent seeds, whether it be flowers or vegetables, are undoubtedly the strongest and most vigorous ones and which they have shown, more than the others, resistance to adversity and challenging climatic conditions.

Concerning the variety of seeds to be taken, collecting different seeds from each type of plant is recommended to guarantee good sowing for the coming season.

As already mentioned, one of the fundamental conditions for proceeding with the collection of the seed is that it is mature; a seed that has not reached adequate development on the plant, in fact, will not be able to guarantee good sprouts.

The appearance of the flower and the plant, which will appear dry while the fruits, on the other hand, will be ripe, also signal that the time has come for the harvest.

The quality of the seeds is also crucial for the health of the fruits and flowers that will be born the following year: the ideal seeds are ripe, healthy, without roughness, and with a beautiful color.

How to Properly Harvest Seeds

Harvesting your seeds is easy. You can get it done in these 5 steps:

1. Choose the Right Timing

We always harvest the seeds when they are ripe. For example, the seeds of many fruits or vegetables sold as food are often not mature and do not germinate if saved.

This is because the golden rule is that it is necessary to allow the fruit and, therefore, the seed to ripen fully.

Since going to seed reduces plant vigor and discourages further flower or fruit/vegetable production, wait until the end of the flowering season to save some flower heads and, consequently, seed.

Collect the seeds or fruits a little at a time when most are ripe. Don't wait for everything to ripen because you risk losing most of the seed to birds (see sunflower plants and goldfinches) or natural dispersion.

But vice versa, don't do it too soon: it is better to let the seeds ripen on the plants until they are almost ready to disperse on their own. In fact, on many plants, the seeds do not ripen all at once (perform a daily check!); for this reason, it may be helpful to tie a small paper bag or a foot of pantyhose on the heads with the seeds to avoid spreading before being able to harvest: this among other things will prevent you from losing seeds that disperse explosively.

2. Let the Plants Go Seeding

Think of a flower as a seed manufactory— that's precisely what it is. First, let the spent flowers on the plant so it can develop seeds, and then let the seeds dry on the plants. Collect them only when they are dehydrated.

3. Clear Pods, Heads, or Capsules

Clear the pods and the heads of the seeds, or clip the seed capsules on a dry and warm day.

Make sure the seeds don't get wet before storing them. Don't forget to put the seeds in containers and label them, especially if you are harvesting distinct types of those.

4. Harvest

Harvesting is the moment when you detach the seeds from their attachments, as everything but the seed itself, such as pods, filaments, or the capsules that contain the seeds.

To take away fly filaments, put the heads in a paper bag that also contains some stones. Then shake the bag. Pour out the contents of the paper bag on a flat surface and let those filaments fly away. You can then pick out the pebbles so that only the seeds are left behind.

Separating pods and capsules from the seeds is also easy. All you need to do is to pry or pinch them open to expose the seeds. You may then screen the content to separate the seeds from the remaining pods.

5. Separate

To aid in separating tiny seeds from the dry inflorescences, it is helpful to place the harvested flower heads in paper bags and shake them: almost all the seeds will split at the bottom, and we could separate them from the other dry parts of the plant.

To separate seeds contained in fleshy fruits (such as tomatoes, cucumbers, and roses), separate the center from the rest.

Put the seed mass and a small amount of hot water into a container/glass.

Let the mix ferment for 2-4 days. Stir every day.

The fermentation process kills the viruses and separates the good seed from the bad seed and also separates the seeds from the remaining fruit pulp without damaging them as we would by any mechanical means.

After 2-4 days, you will find the viable seeds down at the bottom of the container while the pulp and the lousy seed float. Filter the seeds, rinse them to clean them from the rest, and finally, place them on a paper towel to dry. The seeds must, in fact, be kept very dry.

Once they are well dried, they can be placed in the refrigerator, in a cool place, in well-sealed containers: zipped plastic bags, plastic test tubes, or recycled glass/plastic medicine bottles with airtight caps.

However, remember to label the containers with the names of the plants from which we took them and also the date: most of the seeds preserved in this way will remain viable for a few years and can be sown in the most appropriate period based on the temperatures and the time of year.

Harvesting Flowers

Now, let's see how to preserve seeds and bulbs so that they can come back to cheer us up with their scents and colors next spring.

First of all, whether it is flowers, fruit, cereals, or vegetables, in any case, as the oldest agricultural and gardening treatises teach, we must choose the seeds to be preserved from strong and vigorous plants, they must be well made, not wrinkled, of lovely color. They must also be ripe and healthy to be able to maintain themselves for the next sowing.

The seeds must then retain the ability to germinate; here, it depends on the plants: some last longer, while others lose it immediately. Almonds, walnuts, and hazelnuts, for example, lose them after a year. Other seeds generally, after two or three years; cereals generally keep it for a long time. Let's have a look at the flower seeds.

Primrose seeds should be sown immediately, as soon as they are ripe, lily seeds within a few months of harvest, and lupine seeds even a few years later. The seeds of the rose, then, can also doze off for a few years before germinating. Well, it depends!

In summary, it can be said that large seeds are kept well for a long time, less efficiently than the small ones, without food reserves and oilseeds. Whatever the duration, it is inevitable that the capsules containing the seeds or the seeds themselves must be dried in a cool and shady place, never in the sun, so as to complete the maturation little by little. To keep them even better, some suggest washing them first, letting them dry, and then sprinkling them with quicklime, chalk, and ash to protect them, above all, from animals.

We must store the seeds in cool, dry, ventilated places (too hot makes them lose their germinative energy very quickly) so as not to ferment and not be attacked by insects. The most crucial thing, as I said earlier, is to put them in a paper envelope, on which you can write the name of the species, a note on the variety, and the date of collection, and then collect them in a wooden box.

Here's What To Do With Bulbs:

I must say that the bulbs must be removed or not from the earth depending on the type of plant, soil, and climate in which you are located. Early flowering bulbs, or those flowers or plants that bloom in late February or early March, can be left where they are; these are daffodils, tulips, or irises, for example.

Instead, those that flower at the beginning of summer, such as gladioli, Liliaceae, or reeds, fear the cold and could freeze, so it is better to remove them from the ground in autumn or leave them in pots in a cool, dry place, such as the garage or cellar, without watering. For these flowers, you don't have to wait long after the leaves fade and turn yellow to collect the bulbs or move them to a cool, dry place.

Begonias fear frost and must be dug up in autumn as soon as the intense cold arrives. The bulbs are extracted with a transplanter and left to dry in a cool, shady place before putting them back inside, sheltered, until the following spring. The standard fruit crates are ideal for containing bulbs to be preserved since, being airy, they prevent the appearance of mold.

Harvesting Vegetable Seeds

Although all plants have their own characteristics and must be treated differently, some general rules apply to your garden.

First, you must pay close attention to the growth process of your plants. You will have to select the best, most robust, most resistant plants that are more resistant to diseases and climatic changes. Avoid the last fruits or flowers of the season, now weakened.

As we have already mentioned, we advise you to prefer free pollination seeds: in this way, you will be able to obtain plants that are very similar to those from which the seeds were taken. If, on the other hand, you were to take seeds from hybrid plants, expect plants that will not maintain the previous characteristics and will start cross-pollination.

To collect the seeds of vegetables at the right time, one must also pay attention to the climate and the season: in fact, it is not advisable to collect the seeds in the presence of cold and humidity, while a hot and dry period is undoubtedly more favorable.

In the case of vegetables, it is also necessary to take into consideration the differences between the seeds of the various plants, especially as regards the size or consistency of the fruits, which can be dry or fleshy.

In particular, the most delicate seeds that require more attention are those of aubergines, courgettes, and cucumbers, while those of beans, tomatoes, peas, and onions offer exemplary conservation for longer.

When To Collect the Seeds?

Especially for vegetables, we recommend waiting for warm, dry weather. Once the right season has arrived, the best time will be around 10 in the morning, when the dew completely evaporates. To ensure the seed has reached maturity, you can observe the flowers or fruits: the flowers must be dry, while the fruits must be fully ripe. Only at this point will your seeds have taken on all the nutrients necessary to support the germination process that awaits them later. Remember: only a mature seed will guarantee you beautiful sprouts.

The last important tip to follow in this harvesting phase is to collect more seeds for each plant. By doing so, you will be more likely to have excellent sowing.

In short, to harvest the seeds in a perfect way, some conditions are necessary:

observation: we observe the vegetable garden in the growth and production phase so as to be able to select the best plants, those that produce the most beautiful fruits and that have better resisted lousy weather and disease.

maturation of the seed: when collecting the seeds, make sure that they have reached maturity: the flower must be dry or the fruit ripe. Only when the fruit is fully mature or the flower is well dry will the seed have accumulated enough nutrients to support germination.

time of collection: the best time of day to collect seeds is ten in the morning; by this time the dew has evaporated.

PLEASE NOTE: each seedling must be treated differently. Each seed is different from above; some look like petals, others like twigs, and others even like dead worms. It is, therefore, necessary to have clear ideas and carefully check the shape of the seeds of the plants that will be harvested.

Harvesting Lettuce and Tomatoes

Let's start with the lettuce. First, you will have to be very careful in the flowering phase of the plants: in fact, you will have to favor those with a long foliar production phase, periodically collecting the stems and thus preventing the seeds from falling to the ground. The stems must then be dried and left to dry; once dry, you can get the seeds by simply shaking them. The seeds are then left in the sun just for a few days, being careful not to create mold, and then placed in a cool place inside a glass container or paper bag.

As far as tomatoes are concerned, we advise you to collect the seeds of plants that bear fruit early and have a good leaf density. Once you have chosen the tomatoes, cut them in half and squeeze them into a container where you will pour some water. It will then be sufficient for you to leave the container outside for a few days to see mold form on the surface: remove it and recover the seeds that have settled on the bottom. Dry the seeds in a paper bag in your cellar or another cool, dry place.

Harvesting Cucumbers and Pumpkins

To have excellent cucumber seeds, you first have to let the vegetable ripen directly on the plant until the vines are dead. As with courgettes and aubergines, you will need to continue the maturation of the cucumber indoors in a dry and dark place. Once they have become softer, you can cut them and remove the seeds, leaving them to macerate for four days in a container full of water. You will then have to leave them to dry for three weeks.

On the other hand, the pumpkin's seeds must be separated from the pulp and rinsed under cold water. After leaving them to dry, you will have to arrange them on kitchen paper and keep them in a cool place for at least a month.

The seeds of both vegetables must be stored in paper bags and placed in the usually cool and dry cellar.

Harvesting Roses

Not only vegetables: you can also collect and store the seeds of your precious roses. Even rose seeds require some special precautions for their collection and conservation: once the fruits, or rose hips, are fully ripe, it is necessary to open them and extract the seeds, which will be in a state of hibernation.

To awaken them, just keep them relatively humid and at a temperature between 4°C and 10°C, placing them on sawdust in a glass container or in plastic bags. Conservation can take place without problems in the refrigerator, even for several years.

Harvesting Peppers

As for collecting the pepper seeds, the process is straightforward: you will have to wait for the peppers to have a homogeneous color, and, at this point, you can cut them and separate the seeds from the pulp. I advise you to keep the seeds in a glass container in a dry and cool place.

Harvesting Chili Peppers

The chili pepper seeds certainly deserve a separate discussion, as they must be harvested directly from the fruit.

The harvesting operation is effortless: after wearing protective gloves, the chili pepper can be cut at both ends, then cut and open one of the sides with the help of a sharp knife.

Now it will be possible to detach the seeds together with the placenta, which will allow the seeds to ripen at maximum fertility and protect them thanks to the release of Capsaicin essential oil.

After some time, the seeds will have to be detached from the placenta with a light touch of the fingers; at this point, it will be possible to place them in cardboard boxes in a cool, dry place.

Harvesting Melon

The seeds are recovered from melons ready to be eaten, which have a thick, firm but, above all, tasty pulp. If the fruit is good, remove the seed with a spoon and rinse it well with the help of a strainer or colander. Let it dry for a week by placing it on a ceramic plate or on a sheet of waxed paper.

Harvesting Eggplants

Eggplants must be harvested when they are about to detach from the plant.

Pick the eggplants from the best plants when the fruits are about to detach themselves.

Let them ripen in a dark and sheltered place until the skin loses its shine, then cut them and observe the seeds: they are ready when they take on a brown color.

Extract them together with the pulp and pass everything in a potato masher.

Soak the aubergine puree in a bowl full of water, and you will see that the seeds settle to the bottom.

Retrieve the seed and rinse it with warm water; let the seeds dry on a ceramic plate and, occasionally, turn them over.

After 2 -3 days, place them in a paper bag to hang in a dry and ventilated place for two weeks.

Harvesting Zucchini

On healthier and more productive plants, let a courgette develop as much as possible by leaving it on the plant for up to two months, but don't wait for it to soften before harvesting it; remove it from the plant when the fruit is still firm.

Place it for 15-20 days in a dark and sheltered environment to make it ripen further; then, cut it in half along the long side, remove the seeds and rinse them with the help of a strainer.

Finally, let the seeds dry on a plate, or on oiled paper, for two weeks in a shady place.

Even the zucchini must ripen for about twenty days in a dark and sheltered place.

Chapter 4.
SEED SAVING: STORING

In this chapter, we will know how to store the seeds and how to keep them aside so that they can always be ready and ready, even for the following year. Specifically, we will try to understand and learn how and what needs to be done to best preserve the seeds, keeping all their properties intact so that they can remain efficient even for the next sowing.

Let's learn how to store seeds to ensure you have a good supply of high-quality seeds each season.

Primary Tips for Seed Storage

Successful seed storage starts with a good seed; it's just not worth spending time storing non-viable or poor-quality seeds. Do not save seeds from plants that are hybrids, as they may not grow from seeds as inferior to the parents.

Dried seed pods or flower heads can be harvested by drying them in an open paper bag. Shake the bag whenever the seeds have dried sufficiently, and they will pop out of the pod or head.

Remove non-seed material and retain. Scoop the vegetable seeds out of the vegetable, then rinse to remove the pulp or flesh. Put the seeds on a paper towel until dry.

The best way to store the seeds is to place them in airtight glass containers to be stored in a dry, dark and cool place.

With these precautions, tomato seeds will retain their germination capacity for 4 years, melon and pepper seeds for 5 years, and zucchini even for 10. The only exception is eggplant seeds: stored in the fridge at temperatures around 5 °C, they will maintain their vitality for about 5 years.

How to Store Seeds

Learning how to store seeds helps you become a sustainable gardener. The first tip is in the collection. Select healthy, ripe fruits and vegetables to harvest seeds from. Pick the pods when they are grown and dry but just before they open.

Dry the seeds entirely before packing them. The drier the seeds, the longer they will keep. Storing seeds at less than 8% humidity provides optimal long-term seed retention. You can dry seeds or pods in the oven on a baking sheet as long as the temperature is below 100 F. (38 C.).

Store the seeds in a closed container, such as a sealed mason jar. Place a cheesecloth bag of dry powdered milk in the bottom of the pot and place the jar in the refrigerator or freezer for long-term storage of the seeds. Clearly label content and date it. For seeds that will only be stored for one season, place the container in a cool, dark place.

Storing Vegetable Seeds

To have a good sowing and, consequently, a good production, you will have to make sure you keep them in the best possible way.

Here are my recommendations:

- store seeds in paper rather than plastic bags; the latter, in fact, do not facilitate perspiration and could cause mold inside. However, the bags or containers should not be sealed and must be completely dry.
- always label all your seeds so as not to create confusion when planting: write down the name of the plant, the date of harvest, and any other notes
- let the seeds dry in a cool and ventilated place
- after the drying phase, the seeds can be placed in a cellar which, however, maintains a temperature between 5°C and 10°C and is not humid
- Periodically check your seeds and discard any that have rotted or moldy

As often happens in these cases, these are only general rules, while we know that individual plants have different characteristics from each other.

Seed Storage Viability

Properly stored semen will last up to a year. Some seeds can last three to four years, such as:

- asparagus;
- beans;
- broccoli;
- carrots;
- celery;
- leeks;
- peas;
- spinach.

Long-lived seeds include:

- beets;
- chard;
- the bunch of cabbages;
- cucumber;
- radish;
- aubergine;
- lettuce;
- tomato.

The seeds to use faster are:

- corn;
- onion;
- parsley;
- parsnip;
- pepper.

It is always best to use the seed as quickly as possible for the fastest germination and growth.

How Long Do the Seeds Last?

Even if the conservation of the seeds is carried out in the best way, it is possible that some seeds rot or lose their ability to germinate after a certain period of time, with a deadline that varies from plant to plant; generally, the average duration of the seeds is in any case around a couple of years.

In order to always have fresh and fertile seeds, however, it is advisable to always use seeds from the previous year, which are fresher and have a higher germination power.

The seeds of some plants that soon lose their ability to germinate must therefore be used first, such as those of walnuts and hazelnuts,

Likewise, primrose and lily seeds should be used within a few months of harvesting. Seeds with a long life are instead those of cereals, which are kept for a very long time.

If, at the time of their use, the seeds are dry and too old, it is possible to try to restore their original freshness by soaking them in chamomile for half a day.

Where to Store The Seeds

After harvesting, the seeds must be appropriately stored, choosing the right place and environment. To keep the seeds fresh for the entire duration of conservation and to prevent them from molding or fermenting, it is necessary to opt for cool, dry, and well-ventilated areas and possibly in the dark, however taking care to keep the temperature between a minimum of 5°C and a maximum of 10°C.

Absolutely avoid heat and exposure to the sun. The cellar, for example, can be a good storage room for seeds as long as it is not damp.

Once the ideal place has been identified, it is recommended to place the collected seeds in paper bags, never plastic, on which the name of the plant from which the seed was taken, the date of collection, and any notes on the variety to which it belongs must be written.

In any case, the containers must not be sealed to ensure adequate ventilation for the seeds and thus prevent them from rotting.

After packing, you can collect and arrange all the sachets in a wooden box, while it is recommended to periodically check the health and condition of the seeds.

How-To Store the Seeds

Let's start immediately by saying that a lot of patience is needed for the conservation of the seeds. This is the only way to achieve good results. To preserve seeds, the fastest method is to store them in envelopes and seeds. For those who want to eat organic food, the best solution is to plant the seeds in their own garden. In this way, you will save money, and you will also eat organic food. In this guide, we will explain how to store seeds precisely and effectively.

Seed storage requires cool temperatures, low humidity, and little or no light. Every seed is different, so the exact time to store seeds will vary; however, when done correctly, most will last at least a season.

Seeds Labeling

After collecting the seeds, as explained in the previous chapter, here's what to do and remember:

- always label the seeds;
- keep the seeds in paper bags and keep them in a cool, dry, and dark place;
- avoid using plastic bags, as these do not allow the seed to breathe and consequently cause them to mold and rot;
- the cellar is fine for storage, but only if it is not damp;
- at regular intervals during the winter, check the seeds, remove those that are spoiled and have mold;
- a golden rule that applies to all seeds is to let them dry well, in a cool and slightly ventilated place, before storing.

Storing Vegetable Seeds

To keep the seeds well after the summer, it is essential that the containers are perfectly dry and sterile. They must then be labeled and stored in a cool and very dry environment. With the right conditions, the seeds can last for several years.

After the drying phase, make sure that the seeds are not next to any other type of plant debris. Some experts recommend freezing the seeds for three days to destroy any bacterial growth.

Storing Roses

That's how to preserve roses in a proper way:

- you'll need to harvest the fruit, also called rose hips;
- once they are ripe, after that, open the rose hips: inside, you will find the seeds, which, at that time, will be dormant;
- you will therefore have to wake them up by leaving them in an environment with a temperature between 4°C and ten °C and moistening them;
- also, arrange them on sawdust inside a paper bag or glass container
- to keep them in the best possible way, I advise you to keep them inside your refrigerator.

Storing Peppers, Eggplants, and Zucchini

For all three of these vegetables, we advise you to keep the seeds in a glass container to be placed in a dry and cool place. Here are some indicative data to understand how long the seeds will maintain their germination capacity:

- the pepper seeds will last five years;
- the seeds of the eggplant will last five years, but only if stored in the refrigerator at a constant temperature of 5°C;
- zucchini seeds will last ten years;

Storing Lettuce Seeds

Lettuce seeds are self-pollinated. Since the female part of the plant is very close to the male one, a tiny breath of air will suffice to drop the pollen on the receptive stigma. In this case, the seeds will produce the same plants they are derived from.

At the time of flowering of the seedlings, those with a long phase of leaf production and slowness in going to seed should be selected. As the seedlings grow and mature, the stems must be harvested promptly to prevent the seeds from falling to the ground.

At this point, the stems will be left to dry, and once dry, it will be sufficient to shake them to obtain the seeds. They will then have to stay in the sun for a couple of days, taking care to cover them at night to prevent the formation of mold.

Finally, the seeds must be placed in an airtight glass container and placed in the dark in a cool and dry place.

Storing Tomato Seeds

The first recommendation is to select seeds from plants with early fruiting and good leaf density; the seeds must be harvested when they are ripe and when they are becoming soft.

After selecting the tomatoes from which to take the seeds, cut them in half and squeeze them into a jar, then add water to cover the pulp and seeds. Place the jar outside and wait a few days in order: the time necessary for the formation of mold on the surface. At this point, open the jar, remove the mold and recover only the seeds that have settled on the bottom.

Pass through a sieve so as to eliminate any gelatinous residues, and then arrange them on a plate to facilitate drying. When they are perfectly dry, you can place the seeds in envelopes in a container and store them in a cool, dry place.

In short, storing the seeds of your vegetables or flowers is simple and fun. All you need is some methodical order and lots of paper bags, as well as a suitable cellar, but this way, you can keep your favorite crops going year after year..

Chapter 5.
MAKING SEEDS: A PRACTICAL REMINDER TO SELF-PRODUCTION

They talk on many occasions about plants for vegetable gardens and balconies and the techniques for cultivating them and taking care of them in the best possible way in every season of the year. We may not often talk about the most effective practices for self-producing seeds and giving life to new seedlings without resorting to buying seeds in the store. Let's see what to know in this practical step-by-step reminder on how to make your seeds.

Patience

To succeed in this small yet significant initiative, you will undoubtedly need a lot of patience, particular attention to the way you will treat and store the seeds, and some valuable suggestions that will make the task easier for you, especially if you intend to leave by car - production of vegetable seeds.

Variety

Whatever variety you choose - you can select the ones that are most handy, local, and easy to collect and store to start with those, and then proceed with the more complex ones - remember that the degree of germination of the seed - i.e., the ability of the seed to give life to healthy plants.

This parameter depends very much on the conditions of the seed itself, which must always be fresh and kept in a dry place, on the climatic conditions of the surrounding environment, and on the fertility of the land.

Harvesting

The best time to harvest seeds depends on the variety of plants. Plant seeds, such as pumpkins, tomatoes, and melons, should be harvested when fully mature. Beans and peas, on the other hand, should be left on the plant until they are completely dry.

Cleaning

Once you have identified the variety you want to reproduce (pumpkins, courgettes, peppers, chilies, tomatoes, beans, green beans, etc.), proceed with a thorough cleaning of the seeds, on the surface of which there must be no traces of vegetable pulp, filaments or jelly. You can clean with water or dry, rubbing gently with a cotton cloth. Do not neglect this step, as the presence of organic material on the seed could cause mold and rot, which would irreparably compromise the success of sowing.

Germination

If you are not sure of the 'germinative capacity of your seeds,' you can 'measure' it with a little trick: take a handful of seeds (10 are enough), wrap them in two sheets of moistened absorbent paper, place everything in a sealed plastic bag sealed and left to rest in a warm place (near the radiator) for a week. If you find a good number of sprouts when you reopen the bag, it means that your seeds have a satisfactory degree of germination.

Disinfection

It is also vital to make sure that the seed is purified and sterilized inside it from any pathogens: we are talking about the so-called 'sanitization of the seed,' an operation that you can perform naturally and straightforwardly by immersing the clean seeds in a bowl of hot water and leaving to soak for about twenty minutes.

The water must be kept at a constant temperature of 45-50 C°, and the seeds must be placed in cloth bags.

Fermentation

Another method, proper if you are dealing with tomato or cucumber seeds, is fermentation. It is a matter of leaving the seeds to macerate in a glass with a bit of water for 3-4 days and waiting for a white patina to form on the surface (the bacterial load), which you will then remove under running water, using a filter.

Drying

Once cleaned and sanitized, the seed is ready to be dried. This is perhaps the most critical step since it must ensure the perfect removal of humidity from the seeds and thus avoid the formation of dangerous molds.

During the hottest months of the year, it will be sufficient to place the seeds on a sheet of wax paper (so that they do not stick together) and place them in a sufficiently large flat dish. The humidity will be eliminated gradually by evaporation, naturally and relatively quickly. Remember to stir the seeds from time to time.

In winter, on the other hand, drying can be obtained by keeping the seeds in a warm, dry place (on a shelf or in a wardrobe), away from direct heat sources (not in the kitchen!).

In both cases, the drying times vary according to the temperature, the size of the seeds, and the humidity of the air; generally, it ranges from 1 to 2 weeks. To test its dehydration, lightly bite the seed: if no teeth marks remain on the surface, drying will be complete.

Seed Longevity

Seeds can last from two to 10 years, depending on the type of seed and storage conditions. You can verify that your seeds are still good for planting by doing a germination test. If the seeds germinate successfully, then they are ready for another growing season.

Storage

The survival of the seed will significantly depend on how you store it. If you have carried out the previous steps correctly, you will have to hold the seeds in dry and dry places, in well-closed containers, and away from the intrusion of insects or parasites which could affect or even eat them.

BOOK 3:
Seed
Saving & Storing
Advanced Hacks:

A Collection of No-Brainer Methods
to Build Your Seed Bank,
and Live the Frugal Gardening Style.
Amish Tricks Included

Chapter 1.
STORING SEEDS ADVANCED

How are you, future master of seed saving? I am sure that, at this point, your journey to begin to understand the wonderful world of seed saving has already begun! On the other hand, this is not just one of the activities you can carry on or a simple 'hobby' like reading or hiking: seed saving is a noble art that serves many purposes.

The first, logically, is to preserve reproducible material - the seeds, in this case - in order to be able to replant it and see it grow in the following years.

The second, we talked about it extensively in Book 1 of this collection, is to preserve the varieties and strains of the seeds themselves. On the other hand, doing it from a simple pastime born out of curiosity and thirst for knowledge is becoming a real necessity: local varieties, driven by industrialization and mass agricultural standardization, are disappearing.

The third reason, consequently, is to maintain the genetic diversity of each individual strain. Under penalty of the erosion of biodiversity and also the disappearance of mankind - and I'm not exaggerating (for every reference to this concept, to review it and understand the vastness of its implications, I refer you to Book 1)!

Finally, the last reason concerns the cutting of expenses and the consequent economic savings. And here, I want us to stop and reflect for a brief moment.

Without returning to the economic and practical discourse of the costs of registering patents on one's seeds - an issue that many seed savers fight against - we can simply consider the 'philosophical mission' that gave birth to the seed savers network.

Saving money and preparing for any eventuality (even a catastrophe that knocks out the genetic heritage of the seeds) also means sharing: seeds are everyone's right, and it is everyone's duty, instead, to protect and share them.

In this regard, it does not make any sense to buy them from resellers, who charge the products themselves exorbitant costs.

And here we return to the economic discourse: in an age where everyone has difficulties and where the 'general climate' does not promise anything rosy, it is essential to aim for the independence of production and the support of a network of like-minded people... the seed savers, precisely!

So: in Book 2, we saw the cardinal principles of seed saving, starting from the choice of the seed, from its collection, up to the preparation for storage.

In this Book 3, therefore, we are going to understand how to be able to count on effective, advanced, and catastrophe-proof (!) hacks and methods that will allow you to master your seed saving art, live a frugal but full and varied life and cut costs.

Let's take your seed savers experience to the next level!

Chapter 2.
10 HACKS TO KNOW ABOUT SEEDS

Before discovering the foremost advanced and sophisticated methods for saving seeds, it is good to answer some fundamental questions about seeds, clarify any doubts, and bring our experience to a higher level of knowledge and professionalism.

1. Seeds, Living Beings

Each seed is a living being in a state of rest. Even if it doesn't look like it because it has no leaves and doesn't move, it breathes, emits heat, distinguishes between light and dark, and eliminates waste substances.

In short, it is in all respects a living being, however, destined to die when it sprouts to allow the new plant to which it will give rise to living. This is important to know to understand how best to keep it viable and give it the best possible environment until it is placed on the ground.

2. Germinability

A good seed as such must be germinable. If placed in the optimal light, humidity, and temperature conditions, it will germinate and give life to a seedling.

There are seeds, such as those of some aromatic plants (oregano or thyme) or decorative flowers, which need light to germinate and, therefore, must not be sown covered with earth. Just place them on the ground's surface and then press them to adhere. Other seeds, however, need darkness and, therefore, to be buried, like beans.

3. Vitality

Unfortunately, it is not enough that the seeds are only germinable; they must also be endowed with vitality. This property causes them to germinate in the shortest possible time.

It is an important feature because when the seeds are in the ground and are not rich in vitality, they remain there without germinating for too long and become prey to molds or insects. Furthermore, they must respect their natural germination period to better respect the lunar calendar.

Vitality is determined by the age and good conservation of the seeds. But each seed also has its germination period; some are faster than others.

Certainly among the 'laziest' to wake up, there is parsley which normally takes more than 20 days, while the sprinters are certainly endive and radish, which do it in 2 days.

4. Germination Temperatures

Each seed needs three important conditions to germinate: humidity, light, and temperature suited to its requirements.

The ideal temperature for most vegetable seeds is, on average, around 25° C., with celery at the extremes requiring only 20, but only during the day and instead requiring the cooler night, and watermelon, which instead needs requires at least 35.

The seed of each variety of vegetable reacts differently to the stresses of the outside world, a sign that despite the centuries of domestication and selection they received first from farmers and now from geneticists, their original nature has not changed. We should therefore be the ones to adapt to their needs and, first of all, get to know them to promote their growth.

5. F1 Hybrid Seed

When buying sachets of commercial seeds, it is common to find this denomination next to the name of the variety on the sachet. Commercial hybrid seeds are not something modern; they have been around for many years, nor are they something negative in themselves.

This characteristic mainly indicates two things: that the plant comes from the crossing of two pure genetic lines and that it will give a very homogeneous product in terms of shape, height, weight, and flavor. Surely it also indicates that the seed it will produce will be another hybrid seed and, this time, no longer uniform.

If seeds harvested from a tomato or an F1 hybrid melon are reseeded, for example, the plants that will grow from them, this time F2 hybrids, i.e., of the second lineage, will in most cases be different from each other and perhaps not even that much as productive as the mother plant.

This is why reseeding hybrids is usually not recommended. On the other hand, it is wrong to believe that the seeds of hybrids cannot germinate: they are germinable like other non-hybrids, only they may no longer possess all the food and production characteristics of their variety.

We will address this particular topic better in Chapter 4 of this Collection.

6. Seed of Open-Pollinated Varieties

Instead, they are the opposite of hybrids, i.e., the seeds harvested from these varieties are genetically stable and retain all the productive characteristics of the mother plants and, therefore, can be reseeded. They are also usually old traditional varieties and are much cheaper than hybrid seeds because they are easier to grow.

The old varieties have the advantage of not having been subjected to modern techniques of genetic modification; they retain traditional flavors, and they are often more suitable for amateur cultivation because they do not have those characteristics which are useful for the mechanized harvesting system and the cold storage of large-scale retail trade. And in fact, they allow you to cultivate yourself, even the seed, for your consumption.

7. The Best Container To Store Seeds

Seeds often have to stand the test of time, live, and be stored for years before being reseeded. What is the best container to protect them during this storage period? It may seem strange, but the materials that help conservation are certainly the simplest ones: small paper bags, in turn, contained in glass jars or a tin boxes.

The important thing is that the bags have a good seal and do not scatter seeds.

Seed storage requires a dry, dark, and cool place in order not to create suitable conditions for germination. The place must be clean to avoid contact with disease spores and unwanted molds.

How to avoid woodworms? Just mix the seeds with a little uncalcined diatomaceous earth, which acts as a desiccant and a natural insecticide.

And if you have room in a refrigerator, not a sub-zero freezer, that would kill them; you can use it to store mason jars. This would significantly extend the life of our seeds.

8. Dormant Seeds

There are seeds that, once harvested, are not immediately ready to be reseeded. This is the case with some aromatic plants, such as sage or lavender, or wild seeds, such as almost all those wild trees whose seed does not germinate until a few months have passed since the harvest.

To speed up this awakening process, simply put them in the refrigerator and leave them for a few weeks. In the end, the germination becomes normal.

The same heat treatment can work to accelerate the germination of some slow vegetable seeds: they are left in the refrigerator for some time before sowing them in the ground or a seedbed, and a more prompt and uniform germination is obtained.

9. Viviparous Seeds

Some seeds are not real seeds in a state of rest but real live sprouts. This is the case of the agretti roscano seeds, which instead of the seed, actually produce a very small sprout, or the chayote, which is a very large seed inside the fruit and which cannot be separated from it without devitalizing it.

The life of these seeds is usually a few months from the moment of detachment from the mother plant.

10. Freezer for Legumes

Have you ever put pea or chickpea seeds in jars and, after a few months, found a small troop of black insects, the weevils, who are eating them from the inside? Unfortunately, these insects are small beetles born from eggs laid when our legumes are still on the plant.

To defeat them, just place the legumes in the freezer at -20° once dried and collected.

Unlike the smaller seeds, the seeds of legumes are not damaged by freezing them; on the contrary, the cold kills any type of parasite they may contain and will prevent their eggs from hatching. A simple and effective way to combat a common pest of all legumes.

Chapter 3.
NO-BRAINER METHODS FOR MASTER SEED SAVER

Manually Collecting

The seeds are collected manually (for example, for flower seeds) and by beating the bearers of mature seeds. As for cereals, only a small number of species can be harvested directly in the field by harvesting-threshing.

Threshing of Seeds

When the plant reaches maturity, it is common for the seeds to fall by themselves or to be plundered by birds. That is why flower, herb, and vegetable seed carriers are often harvested at an immature stage. They are then left to dry under a tunnel or in a dryer. Once dry, they can be beaten using different machines. This is the case with peas, beans, lettuce, radishes, cabbage, and fennel.

<u>Wet Extraction</u>

In the case of wet seed extraction (e.g., for tomatoes, cucumbers, zucchini, or pumpkins), very ripe fruits must first be opened or crushed manually or with the help of a machine. To detach the seeds from the pulp, fermentation is used, which also favors the maturation of the seed. After a few days, the seeds are washed with plenty of water and finally dried.

<u>Sift, Brush, and Select</u>

The seeds thus collected are then prepared. At first, plant remains, dust, and foreign seeds are removed. Secondly, small and malformed seeds are removed. These steps have the effect of increasing germination and seed dodging capacity.

The most common cleaning methods, if you have budget, are sorting by:

- weight (air separator)
- size (sieve)
- shape (separator)
- specific weight (gravity separator)
- color (visual sorting).

Only the best seeds can pass this rigorous selection to reach the germination test and, eventually, the retail shelves.

Cold Stratification

Many plant and tree seeds, in which winter is an adverse season, do not germinate until they have passed a cold period, also called 'dormancy.'

Seed dormancy is the condition in which a seed cannot germinate, even under ideal growing conditions.

On the other hand, the seeds grow when they are the most likely to flourish. This is because if the young plants germinated in autumn, they could not survive the rigors of winter.

The good news for us serial sowers is that cold stratification, also called vernalization, can be easily replicated with very few objects at our disposal at a temperature of 2-5 degrees.

<u>What You Need for Cold Stratification:</u>

- A fridge
- Some water
- Few sheets of absorbent paper
- A plastic tub (the kind you buy your vegetables in at the supermarket) or a zip-lock bag.
- Some river sand

- Some peat

How To Stratify Seeds for a Spring Planting

We will detail the three methods to simulate cold stratification in nature and thus obtain a high seed germination rate.

1. Procedure with Absorbent Paper Sheets:

This method is one of the most used, thanks to the ease with which you can find the materials directly in your kitchen!

- Soak the seeds for 2-3 hours.
- Dry and spread them on a previously moistened (not wet) paper towel.
- Wrap one sheet of dry paper towel around the other to keep it moist and not too wet.
- Put the paper towel in a zip-lock freezer bag.
- Write the variety and date on the bag.
- Leave the bag in the refrigerator for the necessary time for the species; if the seeds germinate, they should be sown immediately.
- Check once a week that the absorbent paper sheets do not dry out, they must remain moist for the entire procedure, or it will have no effect, and you will have to repeat it.

2. Procedure with River Sand:

- Put some sand in a bowl; it must be enough to keep the seeds apart during stratification.
- Add the seeds to the sand and mix everything.
- Put the mix in a zip bag and seal it.
- Write us the variety and the date.
- Leave the bag in the refrigerator for the species' time; if the seeds germinate, they should be sown immediately.
- The sand must remain moist throughout the treatment; check the bag's contents weekly!

3. Procedure with Peat:

This procedure is very similar to the previous one, but you will use peat which you will surely have more than river sand (not easily available).

- Put some peat in a bowl; it must be enough to separate the seeds during stratification.
- Add the seeds to the peat and mix everything.
- Put the mix in a zip bag and seal it.

- Write us the variety and the date.
- Leave the bag in the refrigerator for the species' time; if the seeds germinate, they should be sown immediately.
- The peat must remain moist throughout the treatment; check the bag's contents weekly!

Sowing After Successful Cold Stratification

The time required for cold stratification will depend on the species itself. Generally, 4/5 weeks are sufficient for most species, but I invite you to check the times on our professional guides written under each product!

When there is no more danger of frost in your area, spread the seeds on the soil as you usually do and keep the soil moist until germination.

Autumn Sowing for a Natural Cold Stratification

For a natural cold stratification, the seeds must be sown in autumn outdoors with these simple steps:

- Use a wooden box or any container available
- Add peat and river sand (75-25%)
- Sow to a depth no more than twice the size of the seed (e.g., 1cm seed, sowing depth 1.5cm).
- Once sown, the substrate must be kept constantly moist.

Spring germination could be homogeneous or slip within a few weeks.

Warm Stratification or Aestivation

Many types of seeds have an induced 'dormancy' and need treatments to remove them.

Dormancy is a condition of stability necessary for seeds to overcome adverse conditions (autumn-winter). This is because if they germinated in autumn through an unexpected heat wave, the young seedlings would die with the arrival of winter.

With hot stratification or aestivation, the seeds are exposed to a temperature of 15-20 degrees in humid conditions.

Usually, the warm stratification is carried out before the cold one to make the seed softer and allow the embryo to ripen; only the mature embryo can 'understand' the subsequent cold stratification process and arrive at germination.

Below I will explain the procedure for carrying out the warm stratification with the materials above to be used, all easy to find.

What You Need:

- Few sheets of absorbent paper
- Some peat or vermiculite
- A plastic tub (the kind you buy your vegetables in at the supermarket) or a zip-lock bag.
- Some water

Procedure:

- Soak the seeds for a couple of hours.
- Fold 4-5 sheets of absorbent paper and place them in the plastic tray.
- Dry and spread the seeds on the sheets of absorbent paper previously wet and squeezed (not wet).
- Place the tray at a temperature of 15-20 degrees, away from direct sunlight.
- In case of later cold stratification, you can use a zip lock bag and fill it with enough soil (wet and squeezed out) to keep the seeds separate.
- Make three holes and leave them at the previously requested temperature. The zip lock bag is chosen because it will then have to be transferred to the refrigerator for subsequent cold stratification.
- Check every week that the soil remains moist; the seeds could germinate, at which point, move them very gently into the containers.

Drying and Storing: Advanced Method

A seed always determines the growth of a plant. This is a small element that, once planted, sprouts and slowly develops its roots. Once it fully expands to produce stem, leaves, flowers, and fruit.

Then, you can develop your seeds. These must be removed from the plant and stored to have new plants. The specific procedure is to dry and store them properly.

I will explain how to dry and preserve the seeds in this paragraph.

What You Need:

- Milk
- Glass or tin containers
- Seeds
- Paper bag

Choose the Right Drying System

Drying the seeds is essential as it helps to preserve them for a long time and free them from any humidity. In summer, just put them on a plate in the sun. To do this, just use wax paper. Instead, you can keep them in paper bags if they are small seeds in winter. Or in hemp bags, if they are large seeds instead. The drying time is determined by various factors; the size of the seeds and the atmospheric conditions. For seeds with a circumference up to 3 mm, two weeks will suffice; for very large ones, it may be useful to try to chew them.

Choose Suitable Containers

Choosing the right containers is essential. Since even if the seeds are not used, it does not mean they are not active. Therefore, the containers must be suitable for conservation and not damage the seeds. For this reason, choose materials such as glass and milk. These must have a lid, which will serve as protection. This way, the light will not penetrate, and the seeds will remain healthy.

Moreover, they keep insects and small animals away. After you get the container, take a paper bag and put the seeds inside. Subsequently, place them in the container and close them with the cap.

Choose the Right Place

Choosing the place to store and dry the seeds is essential. These should be placed in a dark and a little humid place. In this way, you will avoid the proliferation of molds. One of the best methods is to store them in the refrigerator. But, if you need them soon, I suggest you keep them in a cool room with a low and constant temperature. Here's how to dry and store seeds..

The Prepper's Method

If you intend to dry chilies of any kind for their consumption 'in small pieces' or 'powdered,' you must use a dryer, i.e., a household appliance such as this, which in a few hours eliminates all the humidity making the fruits dry and crumbly. Leaving them exposed to the environment for a few hours is enough for the lost moisture to recover, the berries are ground or pulverized, and the product is placed in a humidity-proof container, the classic Mason Jar. However, I do not recommend using a dryer to produce seeds as too high temperatures are reached inside these machines, which can compromise the fertility of the seed.

What follows is the simplest and cheapest method and also the one that allows you to achieve the best results.

What You Need

Few things: a chopping board, an excellent pointed knife, and an 'optional' latex glove (one is enough). If gloves are not used, and very hot peppers are being handled, at the end of the work, it is mandatory to wash your hands carefully several times with 'Marseille' type soap, then dry them and rub a little vinegar over them.

However, be careful to touch your eyes and private parts with hands soaked in Capsaicin, the damage, while not irreversible but only temporary, is very, very annoying.

Saving the Placenta

This is the terminology commonly used to distinguish the different parts that make up a pepper. It is a question of isolating the entire cluster of seeds together with the placenta (the whitish and spongy area where the seeds are attached) from the rest of the pepper (petiole, apex, pulp). Let's start with a Yellow Habanero.

First, remove the stalk, the corolla, and a few millimeters of the upper part of the fruit; insert the tip of the knife into one of the openings between the ribs of the pepper, then make a longitudinal cut to divide two the fruit. The blade must work only on the outside of the chili, being careful not to make incisions on the seeds, which, being fresh, are very tender and vulnerable. Always with the tip of the knife, the whole placenta is removed, complete with seeds, and the game is done.

Why also extract the placenta rather than detach the individual seeds, as almost everyone does?

For two simple reasons:

- when connected to the placenta, the seeds continue to ripen, reaching their maximum fertility potential;
- during the drying phase, the placenta releases the essential oil of Capsaicin on the surface of the seeds, which, among its innumerable properties, constitutes an excellent protective film from external agents; humidity, molds, viruses, bacteria, and anything else will find a practically insurmountable barrier. In practice, the seed is 'encapsulated' and protected in a completely natural way without using particular products on the market and which leaves the time they find. Your seeds will take on a healthy and shiny appearance and be viable for longer.

What About Little Peppers?

Extracting the seeds with the system described above from small berries generally of the C. Annuum species is a bit problematic due to the size; it is better to remove the stalk, corolla, and apex and divide the pepper in two without trying to isolate the placenta and seeds.

Drying

Due to their low fleshiness, the seeds of the chili peppers of the species C. Annuum and C. Baccatum, treated with the method described above, dry quite quickly; just place them on a net like this:

Then place them in a warm and dry place (above a radiator, for example), and they will be ready for storage in a few days. At this point, it will be enough to manipulate them a little with two fingers to drop all the seeds; the remaining placenta, now dry, is no longer needed; it can be thrown away or shredded or pulverized to produce a 'Super Hot' compound as it contains the majority of part of Capsaicin, the element that gives hot peppers their spiciness.

Many believe that the hottest part of the chili pepper is the seeds: nothing could be more wrong; if they are washed by eliminating the placenta residues deposited on them, they are absolutely tasteless and odorless. The seeds, on the other hand, contain vitamins and other substances that are very useful to our body; when producing chili powder, it is advisable to grind the seeds together.

The drying of C. Chinense or Pubescens is instead more demanding due to their fleshiness and high content of oily substances. The advice is to wrap the placenta+seeds in a sheet of kitchen paper which, by extracting most of the juices, will considerably decrease the drying times:

However, do not be in any hurry; the slower the drying, the better the results will be.

The Appearance of the Seeds

Once dried, your seeds should look like this: during the slow drying process, the placenta released its essential oils on the seed's surface, giving it a healthy and shiny appearance in addition to a protective film. The shape of the seed varies according to the species; smooth, clear, and uniform for C. Annuum and C. Baccatum (on the left), more "corrugated" for C. Chinense, even the color takes on slight variations in tone, which recall the chromatic characteristics of the chili from which they come.

Instead, these are to be discarded; the dark spot inside indicates that necrosis of the seed embryo has occurred, useless wasting time, and they absolutely cannot germinate.

They should not be confused with seeds with a dark brownish outline; they are excellent and fertile seeds; this characteristic coloring is typical of the 'Habanero Chocolate' varieties in general.

Seed Storing

You should store the seeds in a dark, cool, and dry place. A cardboard box with a lid and paper bags is the best solution; a handful of rice in the box will help eliminate the little residual moisture. On the other hand, you should not take plastic wrappers and sachets into consideration unless you are sure the seeds are dehydrated.

At room temperature, the seeds will remain fertile for three or more years; as the temperature decreases, the seeds can be stored for tens, hundreds, or thousands of years! If you have a freezer with a constant temperature of -25°C and you hold your seeds in it (they must be completely dry and sealed in a plastic bag with a slider of those series together with a handful of rice) for a thousand years someone will be able to show them, and they will sprout!

Even at a temperature of 5-8°C in the refrigerator, the seeds (and not only those of chili) remain fertile for a few decades (these things are not written on the seed sachets on the market!).

Chapter 4.

SEED LIFE CYCLE AND GERMINATION TEST

While I know you've become a shrewd and dedicated seed saver by now, there may be times when you put your seeds away and forget about them. Or in any case, it's always better to know this technique that I'm about to explain to you... you never know! If you happened to take away and forget about seeds, then, don't throw them away: the longevity of some seeds might surprise you! Even if their use-by date is already past, carry out the germination test. You will probably be stunned at how much life seeds bring with them. Did you know that stored in optimal conditions, tomato seeds remain alive for up to 10 years?

How Long Does The Seed Last?

The useful life of the seeds depends on the plant itself (it depends from species to species, as we already mentioned) and on the conditions in which the seeds have been stored (cool and dry). Although some seeds keep germinating for a long time, it is believed that we should sow no more than two years old in our garden. The best thing is to use the previous year's seeds, which, being fresher, germinate better. However, since our horticultural hearts won't allow us to discard this source of life, we must control them. We check, for example, if the shape of the seeds is not altered (i.e., it is without hollows, without wrinkles, etc. – depending on the seed, of course). Are the seeds still compact and full? Do they look healthy? To get started, this table can help you to check how many years the seeds of some vegetables last:

Vegetable Minimum life cycle in years*:

Vegetable	Life in Years**
Broccoli	3
Brussels sprouts	4
Pumpkin	4
Onion	1
Chicory	4
Black Root	1
Cauliflower	4
Endive	5
Beans	3
Celeriac	3
Mustard	4
Peas	3
Eggplant	4
Chinese cabbage	3
Turnip Cabbage	3
Carrot	3
Fennel	4
Watermelons	5
Cabbage	4
Cabbage leaves	5
Watermelon	4
Nutmeg squash	5
Tetragonia – New Zealand spinach	3
Okra	2
Pepper	2
Tomato	4
Parsnips	1
Leek	2
Beetroot	4
Radish	5
Turnip	4
Sweet corn	2
Lettuce	6
Asparagus	3
Spinach	3
Celery	3

*Source: Ottawa Horticultural Society

**It applies to seeds stored under optimal conditions – in the cold, with adequate humidity, and in the dark. We can verify the germinabilit of the seed with the germination test.

Checking germinability is a very simple process that we can do at home. Let's see how.

What You Need

- standing water or rainwater
- pure cotton gauze or cotton wool or paper used for tea (coffee) filters
- seeds (10 or 20 seeds of the same variety to more easily calculate the germinability as a percentage)
- plate, tray, or another suitable base
- clear plastic film or bag or glass that will make a small greenhouse
- sprayer
- dark paper towel

Germinability Verification Process (e.g., Watermelon Seeds)

In a simple way and with a pinch of common sense: moisten the gauze or paper (with the sprayer), place it on the base you have chosen and arrange the seeds in an orderly manner.

Wrap everything in clear plastic wrap (or cover it with glass) for optimal germination conditions. Then cover everything with a dark cloth or paper to keep the seeds in the dark.

If you verify the germination of seeds of aromatic herbs, flowers, carrots, and parsley, do not cover them, as they germinate in the light. Put everything in a warm place.

The seeds should start germinating after a few days (depending on the plant). Also, check that the gauze or paper is sufficiently moistened and add water if necessary.

If at least 50% of the seeds germinate, the seeds are still alive and can be sown. If the germination rate of the seeds is less than 50%, they are not worth sowing, i.e., you cannot count on them. Also, if the seeds haven't sprouted after two weeks, don't sow them.

If germination is accompanied by grayish mucus coating, the seed is infected with fungi and is unusable.

Where to Store the Seeds

Seed storage requires a dry, dark, and cool place in order not to create suitable conditions for germination. To preserve the seeds, we can use a glass jar with a screw cap (jam jar) or a tin box. The place must be clean to avoid contact with disease spores and unwanted molds.

The seeds from a fresh product must be well-cleaned, washed, and left to air dry before being stored. Do not leave fresh vegetable residue attached to the seed.

Chapter 5.
CHEROKEE PURPLE TOMATO ANCIENT AMISH'S TRICK

They live in an unusual way, which some define as absurd, with out-of-fashion clothes, shaggy beards, and refusing any type of technology, starting with electricity, which is difficult to conceive in our frantic world. But what makes their lifestyle so interesting today beyond the rejection of technology and life so strongly linked to religious tradition?

Their socio-cultural frugal and independent model makes this social group eco-friendly, putting the Amish at the forefront of the most eco-friendly people!

Always, farmers have vital rhythms that flow slowly and steadily, cadenced by the passing of the seasons - as many seed savers do.

Beyond their faith in God, there are two things they believe in: the family (also understood as a community) and working the land, which is challenging but rewarding.

Their plows are pulled by draft horses that consume hay produced by the harvest and whose pollution is equal to the air they breathe, given that the only other waste they produce, feces, is used as fertilizer for the fields.

They raise the animals they feed on naturally so that, in addition to eating healthily, they also have valid helpers in the disposal of daily wet waste.

Moreover, by rejecting modern technology, they have also dismissed GMO crops; year after year, they self-produce the seeds needed for the following season.

A lifestyle that is undoubtedly antiquated but decidedly eco-sustainable, capable of taking and giving to the earth in a harmonious and serene cycle in full respect of its resources.

Just from the Amish, therefore, we take an advanced but very profitable process to save the seeds for the following season.

We start with the technique at the beginning of winter and then store the seeds until they appear the following spring.

Let's have a look by taking the Cherokee purple tomato and the cherry tomato as an example.

<u>What You Need:</u>
- ordinary plant pots;
- some soil;
- a knife;
- some tomatoes from the garden (e.g., Cherokee Purple or cherries);
- a dark and cold place;
- a watering can.

Start this Amish crafting to save tomato seeds, as we said, in early winter. The process replicates what happens to the tomatoes on the plant when they fall to the ground: slowly, fermenting, they transform until they become 'alive.'

<u>The step-by-step procedure</u>
- Take plant pots and fill them with potting soil, leaving 3 inches to the surface.
- Take the tomatoes and cut them with a knife into slices (the same size as the ones you would put in a sandwich).
- Place the slices horizontally on the potting soil, making a couple of layers.
- Repeat this process for each variety of tomato, taking care to use a different pot for each one.

- Once this procedure is complete, head towards the cool and dark place (a cellar, a basement) and place your vases there without touching them.

- In fact, as the Amish themselves say, you can 'forget' about them until spring—they don't need to be treated or watered.

- When spring arrives, therefore, take the pots and place them in the sunlight indoors: do not put them outside, or the external climatic conditions could alter their growth.

- Water the pots regularly, and after some time, you will see the first sprouts appear!

The beauty of this technique, in addition to its simplicity, is that you can get hundreds of tomatoes by slicing and sowing only 1!

Seeing is believing… Amish's honour!

Chapter 6.
BUILDING YOUR OWN SEED BANK

The seedbed is the perfect environment to cultivate our seeds and make our seedlings grow before transplanting them into the garden and creating a scalable gardening system, thanks to which we can also decide to share or sell our seeds.

Let's see how sowing in seedbeds works, the advantages of this type of cultivation, what rules to follow, and how to create a seedbed.

The Advantages of a Seedbed

Transplanting the seedling has several advantages compared to direct sowing in the ground, placing the seed directly in the garden. Here they are:

Fewer fungal diseases and pests. The seed tray allows the seed to germinate in more controlled conditions than in the field. The seedlings grow healthy; the seeds are not eaten or moved by animals and insects.

Save time and better plan. By controlling the temperature, the seedlings develop earlier, and the soil from the garden is used more rationally if it is possible to program the crops. This allows for more crops on the same parcel.

Gaining space in the garden. By transplanting, the area in the garden beds is used better: in fact, by sowing in the open ground, there is a risk that some seeds will not germinate, leaving empty spaces in the rows. The seed tray also saves space even inside the actual seedbed.

Better weed control. When transplanting, developed seedlings are placed in the ground, which finds clean and worked soil. This makes weed control much easier.

Getting Started: What to Sow

While we could grow as many seedlings as we like in seedbeds, some are better suited to transplanting than others.

Cucurbits (pumpkin, zucchini, cucumber, watermelon, melon), peppers, tomatoes, lettuce, and cabbage are the most suitable.

The most difficult ones to transplant, however, are parsley, rocket, peas, beans, carrots, radishes, turnips, and all the seedlings that will have been sown at a well-defined distance.

The Seed Tray

The seed tray is a simple and cheap system; to make it, all you need is a box of inert material (plastic or polystyrene is fine). Wood is less suitable because it absorbs water and can host fungi, while iron rusts and is heavy.

The Loam

For our seed tray, we must use good fine-grained soil: a mix of blond and black peats, pre-fertilized with excellent grain.

Sowing

Fill the box or cells of the trays with potting soil. The planting soil should be slightly wet, not soggy at all. To give dosed water, it is advisable to use a spray bottle. Once the layer of damp earth is ready, the seeds are placed and then coated with a tiny layer of soil. The advice is to lightly press the earth on top of our seeds without compacting too much.

Germination

To germinate, the seed needs only the ideal temperature. The right temperature varies from one vegetable to another; to grow instead, the seedling will need not only heat but also light: for this reason, only the first phase can take place under cover.

After germination, we need to keep our box in an illuminated spot of the seedbed.

Always check that the lighting conditions are correct; if the light is not enough, we will see the seedlings 'spinning', that is, stretching slender upwards and turning yellow due to lack of photosynthesis.

Repotting

When the seedlings have opened the two cotyledonary leaves in our seed tray, it is time to transfer them, planting them in larger pots. As long as the plant has only these first two leaflets, it can be moved without trauma since its small roots are not yet fully developed. When the first real leaves are born, lateral roots are emitted, which could break in the transplant.

The moving operation is called staking and is not difficult to implement: the earth is wetted, and the seedlings are removed with the help of a spoon or teaspoon. Depending on the size of the cells used in the seed tray, all the earth possible is taken, including the roots of the plant, and transferred to a larger pot trying not to damage the roots of the seedling; the operation requires delicacy, given that the young crops have just formed.

After having grown in the seedlings, the seedlings go into jars, which are kept in the seedbed. Here it is expected that the roots wrap around the earthen loaf so that they can be transplanted in the open field without problems.

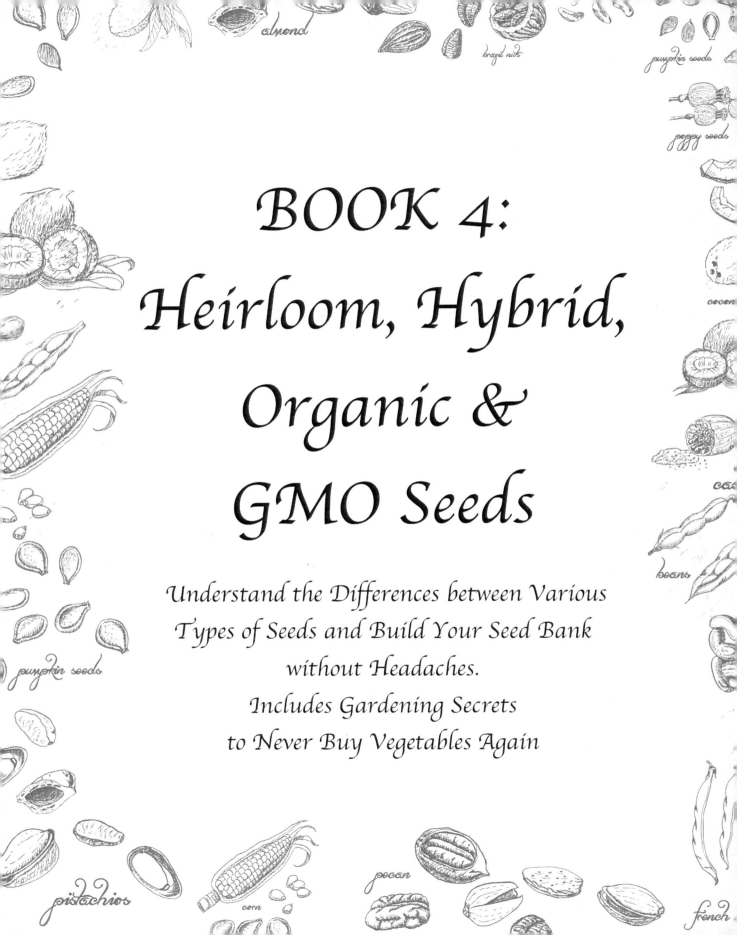

BOOK 4:
Heirloom, Hybrid, Organic & GMO Seeds

Understand the Differences between Various
Types of Seeds and Build Your Seed Bank
without Headaches.
Includes Gardening Secrets
to Never Buy Vegetables Again

Chapter 1.

SEED WAR

There is a great variety of plants worldwide and many types of seeds. These are the last great work of the evolution of vegetable beings since all the genetic information is concentrated in small structures that will make them, if they germinate, become trees, shrubs, palms, herbs, cacti, succulents, etc.

This, if someone does not eat them first, of course, since some are edible, such as sunflower seeds, rice, or lentils, among others. Approaching this world is the most interesting because it will give you a clearer idea of how many seeds there are and which plants produce them.

In this Book 4, on the other hand, we're going to dissect together all the differences between the different types of seeds, giving you all the tools to evaluate which ones you want to approach and how to build your personal garden.

Seeds are an essential part of a plant, not in vain: the genetic material of a possible new generation is just deposited in them.

But they are also crucial for agriculture and horticulture since they are considerably cheaper than a seedling; it is possible to obtain many units that, if viable, will germinate. In this way, we can have a more significant number of exemplars at a low cost.

In this Chapter, we will briefly describe one by one the most frequent types of seeds, to then focus on those that give seed savers the most headaches: Heirloom, Hybrid, Conventional, Organic, and GMO Seeds.

Speaking of the various kinds of seeds, you should know that these are classified into eight groups:

- Baby seeds;
- Creole seeds;
- Edible seeds;
- Flower seeds;
- Fruit seeds;
- Vegetable seeds;
- Improved seeds;
- Hybrid seeds.

Baby Seeds

Its name could already tell you exactly what they are: a kind of treated seed so that the plant remains small once it has sprouted.

Furthermore, these seeds are great for consumption, as they are tender, sweet, and easy to chew. Plus, they have the same nutritional value as the pure ones or even can exceed it.

Creole Seeds

They are the native ones, which have not been genetically modified, at least not artificially. This means that they are the ones that, after pollinating their flowers, plants have produced naturally after being harvested. These seeds come from the same pure species; that is to say, they are not hybrid crosses.

For example, if one poppy (Papaver rhoeas) is crossed with another, your seeds will be the purest.

From my point of view and expertise, having these seeds is the best thing to do to have the certainty that the plants obtained in result will adapt to the conditions of your area.

Edible Seeds

As the name suggests, they are those suitable for consumption and, therefore, those grown for that purpose: sunflower seeds, rice, or lentils, but also pistachios, walnuts, corn, oats, sesame, pumpkin, chia.

While it is true that some can cause some kind of allergic reaction, such as wheat or corn, in sensitive people, in general, we are talking about seeds that, when consumed from time to time, contribute to improving our diet and health. Many are high in protein, vitamins like B or E, and minerals like calcium and iron.

Flower Seeds

Flower seeds are present in different forms: some are so light and small that wind can easily carry them away, such as those of dandelion; there are other larger ones, such as those of rose gardens, that depend more on animals or water, in order to move away from the mother plant.

The color, size, and shape vary significantly from species to species. That's why you have to choose the seedbed well where they will be sown: they need a lot of space to grow.

Fruit Seeds

Like those of flowers, their characteristics vary greatly: those of the cherry tree are brownish in color, rounded, and measure about one centimeter in diameter; those of the fig tree are blackish, elongated, and less than 0.5 centimeters in size.

The plants that produce them are grown in orchards most of the time, but there are also species suitable for cultivation in pots, such as those of the genus Citrus (citrus).

Vegetable Seeds

Vegetables are those plants that are grown for consumption. These include legumes and vegetables, such as lettuce, celery, bell pepper, carrot, etc. All need constant humidity to germinate and often heat, so planting time is usually spring.

Now, to make the most of the season, one can resort to sowing in a protected seedbed or to an electric germinator.

Improved Seeds

These types of seeds are those that have been obtained thanks to a series of techniques and/or processes implemented by human beings and always in a controlled environment.

They have several advantages, as they will sprout plants that are better suited to the environment and more resistant to pests and diseases.

Hybrid Seeds

Hybrid seeds are those that come from crosses of two different species or pure varieties. For example, the seeds obtained from crossing Washingtonia Robusta and Washingtonia Filifera palms are hybrids, giving rise to the Washingtonia Filibusta. These plants have characteristics of both parents but often have one or more enhanced features.

They can therefore be more resistant, produce more fruits and/or with more or fewer seeds, be more resistant to pests and/or diseases, grow faster or have a more or less large adult size.

There are two types of hybrid seeds:

- Free-growing hybrids, which are those that continue to grow after flowering;
- Determined growth hybrids are those that, after flowering, can develop more slowly or even stop growing.

We will talk more about this last type of seeds in the next Chapter.

Chapter 2.
GMO, ORGANIC, HYBRID, OR HEIRLOOM?

After having understood the main characteristics according to which seeds are classified, it is necessary to make a further distinction.

Among other things, concerning the work and study that seed savers do all over the world, the following classification is the most relevant, not only from the point of view of work and practical organization but also, above all, from a political point of view -economic. I'll explain this one better.

So small and light, seeds have been the basis of our livelihood since the dawn of humanity. A seed is a concentration of technology. It is the custodian of the genetic characteristics desired and obtained with great difficulty. Whoever produces, owns, or distributes a seed has a treasure in his hand. The future, although still unknown, is based on present certainties, like the seeds themselves, without which there is no evolution of species and ecosystems.

The first consideration to be made to understand the discourse is, in fact, of a historical nature. The domestication of plants but also with direct reference to seeds established the beginnings of civilization and human society. This 'discovery' is one of the very first technologies that have led to an important cultural evolution of our human species. Cultural, therefore, but not always natural.

All the cultivated or farmed products we know result today from genetic selections, with distant roots, crossings, and reproductions. The concept of the natural has lost its attachment to spontaneous laws, converting itself into exploiting resources.

This happened because, with time and with the development of man, those rites and natural cultivation techniques were lost, according to which the evolution of seed followed the natural rhythms of the cycle of the moon and the seasons, 'imposing' the plants to grow as we decided.

Many seed savers, in this regard, draw a clear line between the seeds before the birth of agriculture - called Heirlooms, which we will talk about in a moment - and all the others, born, raised, and saved afterward.

At this point, a question arises: if this were true, are the seeds we have today all GMOs?

The term GMO (Genetically Modified Organism), generic and popularized by public debate, leaves an indelible stain on which everyone has an opinion, but nobody (or almost) is informed.

Contrary to this line that comes from Heirlooms and reaches GMOs, there are hybrid seeds, born from the union of two pure species, and the organic ones, which for many means 'natural' but which, on the contrary, to be defined such must undergo an important verification process.

Nothing is clear. And that is why I am going to analyze the following types of seeds one by one since, as an expert seed saver, you need to know their differences, modus operandi, and implications:

- GMO seeds;
- Organic seeds;
- Hybrid seeds;
- Heirloom seeds.

Let's find out!

GMO Seeds

Genetically modified organisms (GMOs) are defined as living organisms (plants, animals, bacteria, etc.) whose genetic heritage has been modified by a mechanism other than natural ones.

Regular and widespread monitoring of imported seeds and, in general, of plant material capable of reproducing remains a fundamental point in order to guarantee supply chains that comply with the law. The quality and relevance of the checks for the presence of GMOs arouse great interest from the federal authorities.

Why did that happen in the first place? GMOs find practical applications in food, industry, medicine, and scientific research. The manipulation of the DNA of some plants, such as corn, soybeans, and tomatoes, is used to obtain varieties more resistant to pests and drought.

Therefore, the reason is trivially the following: if a plant 'learns' to become more adaptable to different climatic conditions, it will be able to become stronger and more resistant and bear much more fruit. A logical idea based on intensive agriculture and also of an intensive mind, I would say!

Moreover, there are different types of modifications: do you know the difference between transgenesis, cisgenesis, and gene editing?

Transgenesis is a genetic engineering intervention that transfers a gene that does not belong to the plant and comes from a species that cannot be crossed with it into the plant. The choice, as in the best known and most discussed cases, can fall on genes from bacteria to confer agronomic characteristics (for example, resistance to herbicides) with consequent reduction of the environmental impact or to make it resistant to phytophagous insects.

Conversely, cisgenesis involves transferring a gene in its native form, coming from the same species or from a crossable and sexually compatible species. The result? A product is equivalent to what I could have obtained with a traditional crossing - but in an easier and exact way.

Finally, gene editing, the most popular of which is CRISPR/Cas9, is a different story altogether. It is a 'simple' (even if it has nothing simple) correction of genes through mutations without introducing any external gene. This last method allows one to act on complex characters.

Many experts take sides with particular favor towards this technique, which is undoubtedly less invasive because it does not change the genetic makeup of the species except in a similar way to what spontaneous mutation does. Simply put, a protein cuts DNA at a precise point using a short RNA molecule as a guide to choose the cut point. Editing, with its precision, is proper, for example, for formulating cultures resistant to some pathogens.

The wine sector, which has to use chemistry extensively to combat diseases and climate change, they say, would obtain particular benefits from this type of genetic intervention.

The traditional method of genetic improvement based on crossing and selection is excluded a priori in this field because mixing the genes would create a new variety.

Seed savers, on the other hand, see it differently, preferring those seeds that are not affected by genetic modification processes and, in many cases, even those that were not modified by agriculture hundreds of years ago!

Organic Seeds

The United States Department of Agriculture has established a set of guidelines for defining organic materials, but the lines have been muddled by the introduction of GMO seeds and other altered species. What are organic seeds, then? The unaltered seed that comes from a purely bred plant is an organic seed. Organic seed information comes from US Department of Agriculture guidelines and relies on committed farmers to ensure the seed complies with regulations.

<u>About Organic Seeds</u>

To understand what organic means, you need to know the government definition. That's why the process is not so simple.

Organic recognition follows a set of rules created by a body of our government that deals with all things agriculture: the USDA. Organic gardens must grow plants in a healthy environment with limited and specific chemical use.

A few types of herbicides and pesticides are available to the organic gardener, but the list is short and the methods and amounts of application are limited. The seed of plants grown in the prescribed way can be labeled as organic.

<u>The Rules of Organic Seed Gardening</u>

Organic is a fairly new term in agriculture because traditionally farmers gardened naturally. It's only in the last century that the widespread use of pesticides, herbicides, and unsustainable gardening practices has become commonplace.

Home gardeners tend to follow organic rules only because of the requirement to know what's in their food. Large-scale farmers cannot afford the luxury of manual weeding or non-invasive or integrated pest controls. Agriculture is an activity and is conducted in the most appropriate way, even if not always the most natural.

The seeds from the organic garden cannot come from a farm that has used chemical agents or unsustainable methods. Such production is more expensive, requires more time and effort, and is generally only undertaken by smaller companies. Therefore, organic garden seeds are not as widely available as commercial varieties.

Remember: seeds are just the beginning of the organic gardening process. You need to follow growing practices that avoid chemicals, use natural nutrient-rich soil and chemical-free water to continue the organic path, and ensure your fruits and vegetables are in as natural a state as possible.

Hybrid Seeds

When we speak of 'hybrid seed' (also called F1 or 'first generation'), we mean a particular product that is the fruit of the union between two distinct seeds. Generally, this result is obtained artificially, but grafts are actually also common in nature.

The crossing is usually carried out between species that have excellent characteristics in terms of productivity and resistance to pathogens or between species capable of fighting viruses and species that offer excellent aesthetic results (for example, very red and firm tomatoes).

After years of separate cultivation of the two 'pure' plants, pollination is done manually by crossing the two groups. In this way, the hybrid seed will be obtained.

Indeed, hybrid seeds have essential advantages. The greater and contemporary productivity means that these find increasing employment in industrial agriculture. In recent times, even hobbyists often end up preferring these alternatives. However, the results are not always satisfactory in the face of a more substantial investment.

I will go into detail about the advantages and disadvantages of the hybrid seed for growing tomatoes, chicory, and any other vegetable.

All the Advantages and Disadvantages

The high productivity and resistance of hybrid vegetables

As mentioned in the previous paragraph, the hybrid seed is particularly suitable for industrial agriculture due to the productivity and resistance of the plants. When carefully crossed, the resulting species will be able to bear fruit in abundance and will be better resistant to viruses. This is the reason why many hobby growers now choose to work with hybrid seeds.

Not all pathogens, however, will be duly contained, especially when the goal is to create a plant from which to obtain a high quantity of product.

The Sterility of Hybrid Plants and Costs

The immediately visible disadvantage of hybrid seeds is, on the other hand, their price.

Another limit of no minor importance is undoubtedly the sterility of the plants. In other words, the hybrid seed is unable to produce other hybrid seeds. The farmer will therefore have to continuously buy new seeds if he intends to continue the cultivation.

Finally, due to the production costs, there are few varieties on the market. This can limit the ambitions of all those who have the pleasure of cultivating species that are difficult to buy in the supermarket.

Concentrated and Contemporary Maturation

The last characteristic to consider is the concentrated and contemporary maturation of the plant. This means that the product will be ready in large quantities at the same exact time. Also, by virtue of this aspect, the hybrid seed is ideal for intensive crops that can count on the work of the labor force for harvesting. On the other hand, in private gardens and seed savers communities, there is a tendency to prefer graduated ripening so as to be able to enjoy the fruits of the plant over time and, above all, to be able to complete the harvest without having to face the cost of manpower.

Heirloom Seeds

One of the latest food trends that closely concern the world of seed savers is that of the Heirloom type. In the world of seed saving, this term could not be more precise: it alludes, in fact, to all products deriving from seeds of traditional varieties that are handed down for at least 50 years (but also many more).

Why Do Pure Hard Seed Savers Love Growing Heirloom Seeds?

Because they are different from those we are used to knowing, which could create a much more valuable and tasty crop.

These ingredients are tastier and more genuine than vegetables from large retailers and guarantee genuineness. They are varieties that have resisted all kinds of calamities and infections over the centuries, naturally and independently, by appealing only to their strength.

Furthermore, it goes without saying that from these seeds, products grown without chemical additives are born.

Many seed savers have the habit of exchanging these seeds with each other, consequently supporting local productions and small farmers, who will thus have every interest in continuing production and serving as a virtuous example in the area.

Heirloom also means enhancing vegetables and greens set aside by large retailers for purely quantitative and economic reasons.

A Guarantee for Health and the Environment

According to recent studies, a few days of eating only organic foods would significantly reduce the level of pesticides in the urine. In short, organic and Heirloom rhyme with health, and proposing food of this type means presenting foods free of hydrogenated oils, pesticides, or any trace of human intervention. Buying 'local,' therefore, means supporting the local and regional economy and also reducing the environmental impact of production and distribution processes.

Eating Heirloom products combines attention to health with that of the territory and the enhancement of small farmers and local artisans.

At the same time, that choice allows you to enhance those local supply chains useful for keeping the traditions of a territory alive.

For a seed saver, it represents the pride of representing a family production and a priceless treasure.

Chapter 3.
YOUR SEED BANK WITHOUT HEADACHES

As an attentive, curious, and conscientious seed saver, you may be wondering which seeds to start with to contribute to their constant presence as a global heritage. It is a very intuitive question, but it is difficult to give a detailed answer.

You will understand by yourself that this is a very personal choice for the seed saver, based on his sensitivity, competence, knowledge, and personal decisions.

Yes, because a seed saver always thinks based on the territory in which he lives, above all from a family point of view based on the reproduction and conservation of native species.

The recommendations for the production and use of indigenous wildflower seeds and plantings are intended to conserve our natural flora's biological and genetic diversity.

However, they are mainly based on two points:

- seeds or seedlings used must come from the same biogeographical region where the final parcel is located;

- the ecological requirements of the species used must coincide with those of the site to be greened.

Indeed, the seed mixtures mustn't contain rare or threatened species or species with a discontinuous distribution. The species' natural range is maintained, and the introduction of species into regions where they were absent should be avoided.

The increase in the demand for wildflower seeds has made it possible to develop different mixtures whose composition responds to various ecological situations of the single territory, and this is undoubtedly significant progress compared to the initial condition.

Nevertheless, it is also noted that the 'biogeographical region' criterion is not respected and that the blends offered on the market include several ecotypes of different origins. Consequently, we can fear crossings between autochthonous and introduced ecotypes; this causes a loss of local adaptation and biological and genetic diversity.

Pro Tip: To better respond to the recommendations for seed production, leaving aside the commercial chain and focusing on our seed saving activity, I leave you the following advice:

- Limiting the number of species in the blends, makes it possible to no more extended mix ecotypes but also to offer in the retail trade blends suitable for a defined biogeographical region;
- Encourage the exchange of ecotypes between the producing industries;
- Promote local seeds, introducing only part of the basic mixture;
- Develop the use of seed grass (especially in mountain regions);
- Remove all rare or endangered species from the mixes offered on the market;
- Encourage municipalities to develop blends for green spaces and private gardens in collaboration with the manufacturing industry.

What Seeds Can Be Saved?

Aside from the politics, capitalism, and biotechnology topics that are making headlines, and we have addressed a lot in the course of this collection, the underlying reason why you decide to save the seeds and deepen this noble activity is that you have fallen in love with a plant and its flavor. You want it to grow again, preventing it from disappearing.

It could be the perfect bluebell, the tastiest tomato, or a champion squash. You never know when a seed is in actual danger. Saving your seed is the only guarantee.

Moreover, self-pollinated or heirloom plants are the only two varieties that will grow from seed, meaning the seedlings will look exactly like the parents. These are seeds worth taking care of and saving.

Seeds that have been hybridized (F1) will grow into different varieties of plants with some characteristics of one or both parents. Many, if not most, of the plants sold now are hybrids.

Hybridization can create a plant with desirable traits and offers some job security for the seed company. Saving seeds isn't an option with combinations unless you're looking to discover something new. You could, however, try taking cuttings.

Also, insect- or wind-pollinated plants may have cross-pollinated with plants of another variety, and again, this won't become true. Saving the seeds of these plants requires a little extra attention: that's why sharing these seeds has given birth to the phenomenon of seed savers.

Self-pollinated plants, on the other hand, are the easiest to save. Those include chicory, beans, endive, lettuce, peas, and tomatoes. You can also save lots of heirloom flower seeds like cleome, foxglove, hollyhock, nasturtium, and sweet pea.

Saving Seed from Cross-Pollinating Plants

To obtain pure seeds from plants that cross-pollinate with others of their own species, it will be necessary to physically separate the different species from each other. You can achieve this by:

- planting only one variety of one species;
- planting different varieties at a distance from each other. Different plants require different spaces and can be considerable. Peppers require about 500 yards, and squash plants would need half a mile;
- choosing varieties of plants that flower at different times;
- using a physical barrier, such as a cover or bag. You should cover one variety at a time.

Best Practises

As seen in the previous books, always choose the best quality plants, fruits, flowers, and vegetables to save seeds.

Look for resistance, disease, vigor, great flavor, and productivity. Next year's plants will be as good as this year's seed.

Growing plants from seeds saved from your personal garden will, over the years, be shown in plants uniquely adapted to your garden.

Think about it; seeds are probably the only heirloom that gets more valuable with use!

Chapter 4.
SECRET GARDENING HACKS

Now that we know all about the processes of harvesting, storing, and sharing seeds and have gutted them in all their types, let's go and discover the best secrets for their sowing... even if we're going to dissect this topic throughout the Book 5 of this Collection.

Sowing consists of placing the seeds in conditions to allow them to germinate and subsequently develop. Depending on the species and the cultivation area, sowing can occur in different seasons.

Generally, for the species, woody sowing is done from autumn to spring (November-April), depending on the conditions, climate, and the techniques used. Seeding can be done in several ways:

- outdoors (in open ground, in porches, seedbeds, in containers);

- in a protected environment (in boxes or seedbeds, containers).

Sowing, both outdoors and in a protected environment, can take place by broadcast or in rows. In the latter case, they usually result in the subsequent cultivation treatments being easier, particularly the control of weeds.

Sowing outdoors generally takes place on agricultural land, possibly amended with materials that improve its performance and physical characteristics (softness). Substrates are often used for sowing in trays or containers specially prepared, generally based on peat. The use of sand (river, washed) or sand is frequent for caissons that host forest species with recalcitrant seeds, or that need chilling (e.g., chestnut, oak, walnut, hazel, cherry, field maple, ash, etc.).

Sandwich Sowing

It is a sowing technique generally adopted for conifers if the land is unsuitable and subject to compaction. On top of the properly prepared soil lay one layer of sand of about 2 cm, on which the seeds are placed and then covered with another layer of sand, suitably rolled to compact it slightly. The sand ensures better drainage and a lower incidence of fungal diseases. Subsequent careful irrigations must guarantee the maintenance of a sufficient degree of humidity of the substrate, primarily until the roots of the seedlings have reached the ground below.

For sowing in containers, the substrate used is generally prepared from sphagnum peat. Other ameliorating or corrective substances can be added, such as sand, clay, perlite, vermiculite, wool rock, pumice, volcanic lapillus, compost, loams, etc. The goal is to obtain a suitable substrate, in particular, to ensure:

- good drainage and good aeration (deriving from good porosity and softness);

- maintenance of the volume (i.e., of the porous structure);

- water retention capacity, good absorbency;

- the absence of weed seeds, pathogens, and parasites;

- a balanced nutritional intake;

- low cost.

The most commonly used containers or photocells are plastic pots or seed tray alveolar (multiport), having different shapes and capacities depending on the peculiar characteristics and needs of the species in question and the residence time of the seedlings in the container itself. In particular, the account is taken of the development characteristics of the root system so that it can develop suitably without suffering malformations that compromise its future development.

Studies and recent experiences have shown that vases or containers with a truncated pyramid shape are preferable compared to those with a cylindrical or truncated cone shape; together with other precautions, such as the presence of details ribs in the inner walls of the vase, the convexity of the bottom, etc., favor a harmonious development of a fasciculate root system. It is possible to avoid or limit the inconvenience of the conformation 'nest' of the roots; this constitutes an essential premise for the subsequent post-transplant development of the plant itself.

Compared to sowing in the ground or boxes, sowing in containers allows you to obtain seedlings (seedlings) provided with earthen bread; these seedlings offer considerable advantages: they can be transplanted into a nursery or planted at any time of the year; if well grown, unlike bare root plants they must not undergo cutting of the roots and keep the root hairs intact; they will be able to overcome so brilliantly the delicate moment of the transplant.

The seedlings obtained outdoors have the advantage of being better prepared for the natural climatic conditions they will find following the transplant compared to the seedlings produced in a protected environment, which could require gradual acclimatization.

The permanence of the seedlings in the seedbed can last up to two years. The seedlings obtained by sowing in caissons (seedbeds) or the ground can be potted in the spring following sowing or, if necessary, be thinned out to allow for balanced development. The following autumn, they are ready to transplant (= one-year-old seedlings or S1). If, from the time of sowing to that of subsequent transplant, two years pass, the plants may also undergo a cut of the epigeal part in order to obtain a better-shaped stem or to favor the development of more branches (bushy plants).

Cure for Seedlings

During the period of stay in the seedbeds, the seedlings may need cultural treatments, such as:

- irrigations;
- weed control (the use of chemical herbicides is still problematic);
- fertilizations;
- fight against parasites (e.g., anticryptogamic interventions, against powdery mildew on oaks, maples, hornbeams; interventions;
- insecticides against weevils, etc.);
- hoeing, weeding, etc.

Young plants (depending on the species) often need shading, not liking the excessive irradiation of the summer months. For this, the seedlings are usually kept in spaces protected by nets shading, which also acts as anti-hail nets. With the uprooting from the seedbed, the breaking of the finest roots and of the taproot is frequent. As a consequence, breaking the taproot leads to the early formation of a fasciculate root system. An apparatus at the root of this type is a good premise for easier and safer planting.

Undercutting

It is an operation that consists of cutting the taproot from the seedlings to favor the formation of a fasciculate root system. It is generally carried out on deciduous trees, passing with a towed implement from a tractor with a horizontal blade that cuts the taproot. This operation should be performed for about a month before the vegetative restart (N.B., the radical activity begins 10-20 days before the vegetative restart) in order not to cause excessive stress to the plant.

Chapter 5.
FINAL TIPS TO GROW YOUR VEGETABLE GARDEN

The vegetable garden can be improvised, but with good preparation before the start of the season, we can avoid many problems and illnesses and have better results. Every year, January and February would be the time to plan the vegetable garden. Here are six steps to prepare the vegetable garden easily.

When making your new garden plan, don't forget the flowers to attract pollinators.

<u>Six Steps to Plan Your Vegetable Garden Every Winter:</u>

1. We look at the seed stocks first and throw away the old seeds. We also take into account the level of satisfaction with certain varieties;
2. We find sketches of our garden from past years to respect them during the rotation;

3. On paper or the computer, we prepare the sketch of this year's garden. We indicate the cardinal points, the parts exposed to the sun and the shade, the cold areas, and the morning frost. On the sketch, we first indicate the perennials and the plants that spend the winter in the garden; then, according to the rotation rules, we plan the location of the central plants and supplementary crops;

4. We also plan the time, so that the flower beds are not empty. Between slow-growing plants (cabbage, broccoli), you can sow intermediate crops (lettuce, spinach). It is recommended that the beds are between 100 and 120 cm in size;

5. Depending on stocks and the garden sketch, we prepare the list of seeds and seedlings (varieties and quantities) to purchase. Let's not forget about the seeds of valuable flowers!

6. During the year, we write down the observations valuable to us in planning for the following year.

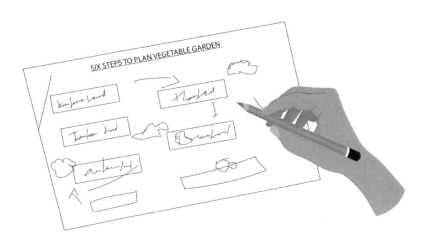

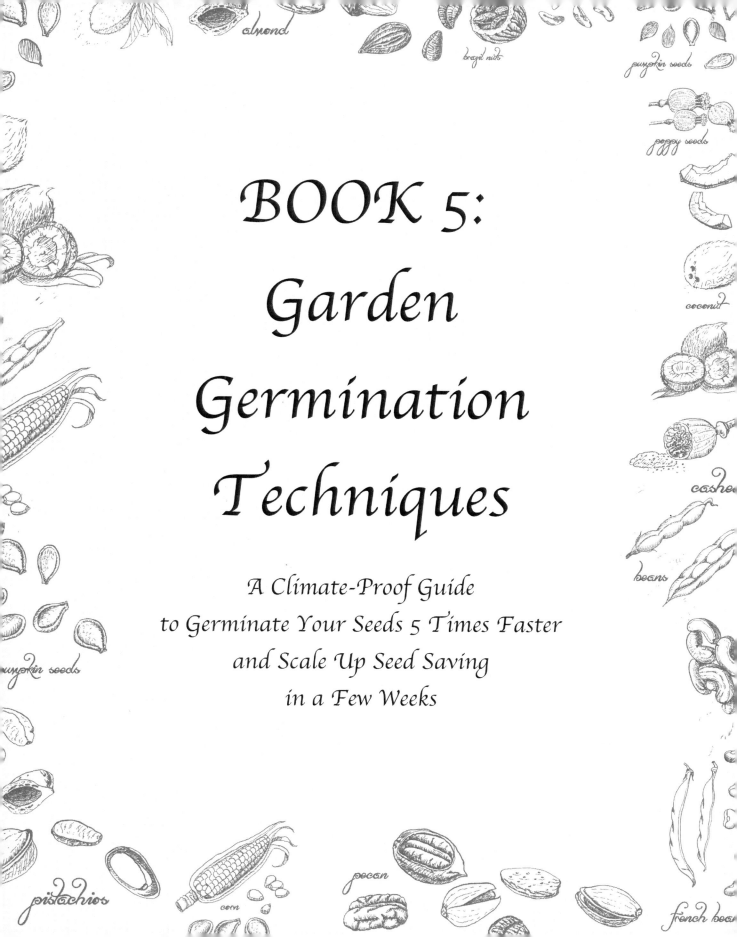

BOOK 5: Garden Germination Techniques

A Climate-Proof Guide
to Germinate Your Seeds 5 Times Faster
and Scale Up Seed Saving
in a Few Weeks

Chapter 1.
GERMINATION: A CLOSER LOOK

Although we have talked about it extensively in previous books, in this Book 5, we will focus on one of the crucial phases of the process of saving seeds: germination. On the other hand, a true seed saver knows how important it is to restore the seed to its splendor in order to build a beautiful, high-quality, and above all, sustainable vegetable garden.

Let's find out together how to do it, starting from the germination of the seeds.

Germination is the development of seeds into seedlings. It begins when the seeds become active and ends when the first leaflets of the new plant appear.

After sowing, the dehydrated seeds enter a period of quiescence. Subsequently, if the times and conditions are favorable, the germination process begins.

Germination is conditioned by the temperature and availability of water, oxygen, and light.

The embryo has the embryonic leaflets (cotyledons) attached to a central axis:

- the upper part of the axis is made up of the epicotyl, which has a feather at the apex (embryonic bud);

- the lower part of the axis is formed by a hypocotyl and a radicle (embryonic root).

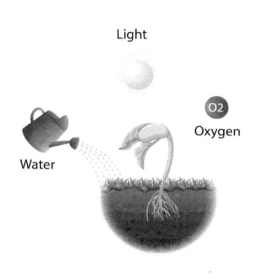

In the early stages of germination, the seed absorbs water; the embryo begins to use its reserve substances, and the radicle swells, breaks the integument, and grows downwards.

Germination then continues in two different ways, depending on the type of seed:

In aboveground germination, the hypocotyl elongates, pushing the plumage and protective cotyledon out of the ground;

In hypogeal germination, the cotyledons remain underground, and the epicotyl lengthens, making the plumage upwards.

The seeds are often found to be significantly dehydrated, with even shallow water contents. This is useful for their shelf life, as they are more difficult to be attacked by molds (fungi) and bacteria, and the metabolic processes are considerably slowed down. This is why the seeds of the most common agricultural species are collected, stored, and marketed only if they have a suitable humidity, generally never higher than 13%.

Dormancy

In addition to quiescence, determined by environmental conditions that are not favorable for germination, dormancy can be found in seeds.

It is a phenomenon that occurs due to a physical or chemical nature internal to the seed itself, inhibiting its germination.

Among the types (causes) of dormancy itself, we find:

- embryonic dormancy;
- enforced dormancy.

Moreover, dormancy can be imposed by the following factors:

- impermeability of the integuments;
- immaturity of the embryo;
- metabolic block;
- biochemical nature;
- a combination of two or more of these factors.

Among the physical factors determining the dormancy of the seeds, there may be the impermeability of the integuments, which in some cases can constitute a mechanical barrier that prevents the absorption of water or gaseous exchanges with the outside. In this way, the seeds retain the possibility of germinating even for many years, and therefore the species can survive difficult conditions for long periods.

If for agriculture this can represent an inconvenience, it represents a survival mechanism for the species. However, it can be reduced or eliminated with practices such as scarification. This operation damages the integuments of the seeds with aggressive substances (acids, bases) or with abrasions or incisions on the integument.

Chemical (or embryonic) dormancy, also called cold requirement, is due to particular substances inside the seed, which act as inhibitors. The progressive degradation of these inhibitors overcomes this phenomenon.

Seed savers can artificially remove dormancy by keeping the seeds at low temperatures (2-10 °C); this practice, called vernalization or chilling, can be applied for a duration variable, depending on species and variety (e.g., 30-60 or more days).

Stratification

There is also an agronomic practice, stratification, which consists in mixing the dormant seeds with moist sand (or sand mixed with peat) by keeping them in a cold environment during the winter and then sowing them at the time of germination. Seed treatments with plant growth regulators (e.g., gibberellic acid) can also result very effective for some species.

Hypogeal (A) and Epigeal Germination (B)

In hypogeal germination (e.g., broad beans), the bud comes out of the ground, the radicle comes out of the integument, and the cotyledons remain under the surface of the ground, supplying the seedling with nutrients.

Subsequently, leaflets will appear, and a lateral root system will develop.

In epigeal germination (e.g., bean), the integument that covers the seed opens; the hook-shaped hypocotyl protrudes from the ground. Subsequently, the hypocotyl straightens and elongates, further pushing leaves and cotyledons out of the ground. The cotyledons will protect the first leaflet.

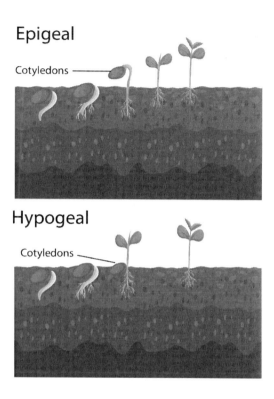

Chapter 2.
GERMINATION: BACK TO BASICS

All plants start as a valuable seed. We saw it well in Chapters 2 and 3 of this collection. And, with that, also a good germination process. After all, during this phase, this 'food' is converted into sugars, which the plant uses to break its shell and form its roots. From then on, the seedling mostly depends on its environment to create the nutrients it will need to survive.

Germination, in fact, brings a seed out of its slumber and starts the growth process. A seed will begin to germinate once it receives enough nutrients and moisture. Then, it will increase in size and open its shell.

A germinal opening is formed and a root will emerge from it; that will help the plant absorb nutrients from the earth. Gravity and Nature ensure that the root grows downwards while the stem upwards, creating a young seedling that can survive earth and light.

So, many people and seed savers want to know how to identify a healthy seed. Honestly, it's always hard to tell if a species will be healthy based on its seed alone. There are, however, some indicative signs. Make sure to collect all the info in Chapter 2 and 3 of this collection.

If you can't use up all of your seeds, store them in a cool, dark, dry place while you can. A refrigerator is ideal.

Planning for Germination

Seeds are designed to germinate, but are more likely to do so if provided with the ideal environment.

There are many germination methods (we will see them all in a moment), but they all need:

- Moisture to help the seed grow and break through its shell;
- Minimal interference so delicate structures are not accidentally broken;
- Temperatures that mimic spring 20° -22°.

If you remember these 3 things, your germination attempts are more likely to be successful.

The first leaves of a seedling after the cotyledons

It goes without saying that successful germination is crucial for your new and upcoming activity or business.

Your seeds are the foundation for your plants, which is why many successful seed savers choose to start with high-quality seeds. You can also improve your germination attempts by using seedboosters, greenhouses and germination media such as jiffy pads.

3 Basic and Easy Ways to Germinate Your Seeds

The top germination method is the one that suits you the most, and if you're like me, you'll want something natural, simple, and sustainable.

My favorite way is a 24 hour soak and then soil germination; still, you may prefear something else for obvious reasons carries a decent failure rate. Here are 3 of the basic and easiest ways to germinate seeds.

Germinate the Seeds Directly in the Ground

Planting your seeds in the soil where you intend to grow is the most common though not the most successful method for all seeds (for example, marijuana seeds.)

That method is perfect for ensuring young seeds have minimal interference as the tiny root is protected by the soil. It is also the most natural way to grow marijuana plants.

When using soil, first make sure you're using the right type. Preferably use lightly fertilized and new potting soil. It should have a PH around 5.5/6.5. This soil will have minerals and spores that help young plants thrive. Do not add nutrients at first, the potting soil has enough nutrients for about two weeks of plant life. If you add other nutrients, you may put at risk your seeds due to nutrient overdose.

To prepare the soil for the seed, create a small hole in it by pushing your finger up to 1.5 cm deep. You can use a pen or pencil too.

Place a seed in the prepared hole and cover it with earth. If you have already germinated, the seed will have a root: position the root facing downwards (we will discuss later on). After covering the seed with potting soil. So beware that means pushing it further down inevitably as you put water in it (you can use a plant sprayer to moisten the soil.)

Do not use a cold windowsill, as the temperature is not high enough for germination. The ground temperature should be 22°.

Keep monitoring your soil to make sure it stays moist. Within a week (or a minimum of 4 days) you should start to see stems emerge from the ground.

Now you have a seedling! Once your plants are 5 to 10 inches tall, transplant them into a larger pot. Your plant will now have plenty of roots that will help it grow it for the rest of its life!

Germinate the Seeds in Water

Germinating in water may seem like a bad idea, as there is more light and water than recommended, but it works! It is around 90% effective. The 'trick' is not to leave the seeds for too long. Usually, it takes 24-48 hours for the seeds to show their tails, but you can let them soak for up to 7 days without too much concern.

However, we always recommend using this method only when you have a good experience.

To the neophyte, we can instead say that soaking the seeds for a few hours before putting them back to germinate in a safer place (discs or germination cubes) could help the seed germinate because it softens the hardest part of the seed.

When germinating in water, the seeds will sink to the bottom once they are soaked.

Water germinating is beneficial because it ensures that there is just the right amount of moisture to start germinating. When done for a short time, it can help crack the shell, causing the plant to pop out before your eyes. In water, germination shortens the process making it lighter for the plant rather than pushing through the soil.

To sprout with water, fill a glass and let it come to room temperature, leaving it for a few hours. The temperature should be around 18°. Do not add nutrients. Refill it with fresh water every following day while maintaining the temperature.

After about 2 to 5 days, the seeds should start to crack. You can place your seeds in the ground anywhere, but once the roots are 3 to 5 mm (0.1 to 0.2 in) long, they need to be planted.

As much as I myself prefer to germinate my seeds in water, it has an added drawback. At some point, you will have to handle your seeds, and that is risky. The germinating seeds are delicate, and the roots are particularly fragile. If you damage them in any way, your plant may not develop well. Be very careful when placing the sprouted seed into the ground, and place the root side down if possible.

Germinate with Cotton Pads or Absorbent Paper

Another easy way to germinate your seeds is to use cotton pads or paper towels. This is a common and basic way of doing it because cotton can keep the seeds protected and moist.

While cotton balls (or pellets) are best for this method, inexpensive, non-porous paper towels will do as well. Just make sure they're plain, single-ply paper towels – cloth-like ones could grow your roots into the towel.

To germinate in a proper way using cotton pads, place a few seeds between two pads and moisten with a sprayer.

When using a paper towel, place the seeds between two paper towels and store the towel-padded seeds between two plates, under an inverted bowl, or in a plastic bag. Keep the temperature around 22° and (again) don't place the seeds on a windowsill.

In about 2-5 days, the seeds will begin to split and a small root should appear. Put them in the ground when they are 3-5mm long.

This method has also some risks. You can damage the fragile roots as you dig them into the ground.

Use gloved fingers or tweezers to move delicate shoots, and don't let the root grow too long before moving it into the soil.

Other Methods of Germination

These 3 methods - water, soil, and cotton pads are the easiest ways to germinate your seeds, but they're not the only ones. We will dig in - litterally - in the next Chapter.

Chapter 3.
GARDEN GERMINATION: ADVANCED TECHNIQUES

Seed Germination in Rockwool

Rockwool provides the perfect environment for seed germination. It is mineral wool made from volcanic rock and other materials (such as basalt and limestone). Rockwool is man-made by melting its ingredients into molten lava that is rapidly spun into threads. These threads are then compacted, cured, and cut.

Rockwool is an ideal growing medium but will need to be modified slightly for plants. First off, you'll need to lower or higher the pH of your plants, as Rockwools have a pH of 7.0, which is too high for germination. To lower the pH, soak the Rockwool cubes in water for at least a day with a pH of 5.5; this will reduce the number.

It should also be noted that there are other drawbacks to using rockwool. Because it doesn't occur naturally, it's not the best for the environment. It's also not the best for your health; wear gloves and cover your mouth and eyes when handling this stuff.

Aside from the extra steps involved (like pH adjustment), the material is very affordable and easy to find. Since it does not require soil, this method is ideal for those intending to grow it hydroponically, but, of course, it is also suitable for subsequent planting in the ground.

Prepare Cubes for Indoor Germination

These three tools are essential for germination and must be used with care since seed germination is a delicate moment in the life cycle of the plant:

- Mini greenhouse (in which to germinate the seeds);

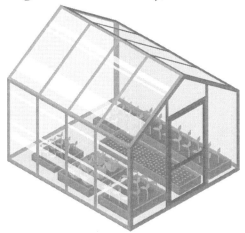

- Rockwool cubes (at least 1 for each seed you want to germinate);

- Root Stimulator (the fertilizer).

<u>Start at the Mini-Greenhouse</u>

In summary, for germination, a controlled environment is needed, where there are adequate temperature and humidity: the mini-greenhouse where to insert the seeds to be germinated or the containers for sowing.

Each seed is inserted into a single rockwool cube. Finally, a root stimulator which is basically a typical fertilizer or nutrient in the hydroponic technique.

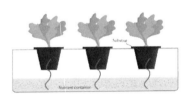
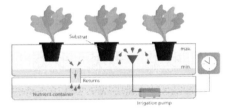
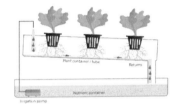

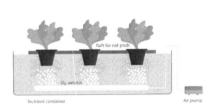
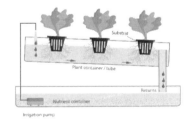
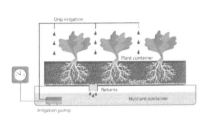

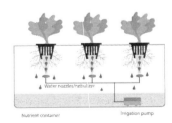

Germinate in Rockwool Cubes

In this section, we explain how to germinate seeds to get sprouts and start growing indoors. To properly prepare your germination area, you need to have:

- cubes or disks for germination;

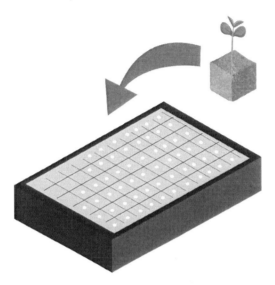

- root stimulator to quickly develop the root system of plants.

To prepare the germination area, it is necessary to have cubes of Rockwool and the root booster, to quickly develop the root system of the plants.

Below we illustrate the characteristics and the procedure to start - step by step - the germination phase in Rockwool cubes:

Prepare a solution with 5 liters of water and 20 ml of Rootbooster Cellmax root stimulator or an equivalent product.

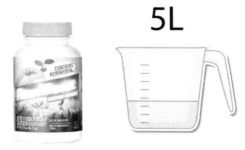

Take the Rockwool cubes and leave them to soak for about 24 hours in the solution of water and Rootbooster to make the Rockwool cubes less alkaline (their pH tends to be 7.0).

The following day, drain the cubes. Rockwool cubes retain a lot of water, so it is useful to drain the Rockwool cube to allow a correct exchange of water and oxygen.

Insert the seed in the appropriate hole (of the Rockwool cube) at a depth of 1/2 (half) cm.

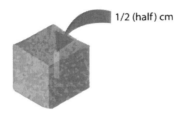

Insert the cubes inside the mini-greenhouse and keep the temperature at about 25/26°C with a high humidity rate (about 80%).

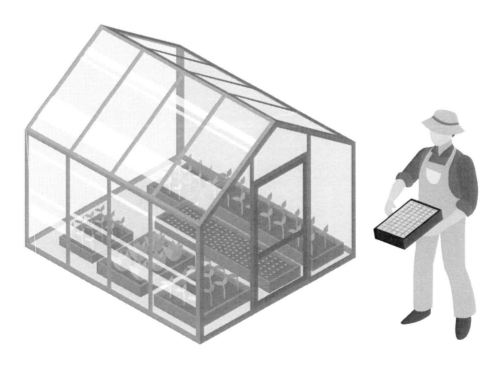

Bring the neon lamp close and keep it on 24 hours a day (when the seedling starts to emerge).

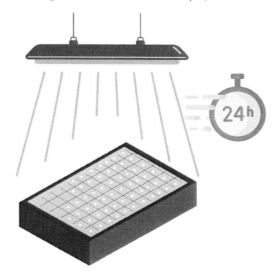

<u>Pro Note:</u> the seed initially does not need too strong light. Once the seedling has popped out of the Rockwool cube, however, it is essential to illuminate it with delicate light (preferably using a neon type light, or HPS and/or MH lamp (monitoring temperature and humidity). The seedlings that do not receive adequate light tend to have a very long stems. Depending on the type, quality, and age of the seeds, germination can take anywhere from 2 to 14 days.

Once the roots have passed through the Rockwool cube, they will tend to come out of the sides and bottom of the cube.

The germinating seed is very delicate and should not be touched.

Seed Germination in Jiffy Peat Discs

Jiffy pads are peat pellets, another way to germinate seeds without the risk of damaging young roots. Peat pellets are made from compressed peat, partially decomposed plant matter, and are simply delicious for young plants.

The pellet enlarges as water is added, forming a container of nutrient-dense soil around the germinating seeds.

Unlike rockwool, peat is already optimized for cannabis germination. It has a pH of 5.5, so you don't have to worry about making any changes. The only preparation required is to soak the pellet in water. Once the roots become visible (popping out of the peat), simply move the entire shell into the soil, rockwool, or coco coir, where it will continue to grow.

This type of germination is not recommended for hydroponic cultivation.

Peat pellets have a good germination rate, are easy to use, and are suitable for beginners.

Preparation of Jiffy Disks

Prepare the solution with water and a root stimulator such as (Cellmax Rootbooster).

Immerse Jiffy disks in the solution for a few minutes (10/15) until the disks are visually inflated.

Drain them from the excess solution and place them inside the mini-greenhouse.

Insert the seed into the Jiffy disk. Make sure to insert the seed a few millimeters below the surface of the disk (4/5) mm.

How to Optimize the Process?

Once the seed has been inserted, place the disk in a mini greenhouse. Inside the mini greenhouse, temperature and humidity are two very vital factors. We recommend maintaining a temperature of around 26 degrees and very high humidity of around 80%.

To guarantee the correct humidity and temperature, it is possible to associate a heating mat or a heating cable with a thermostat to the mini-greenhouse.

When the sprout comes out of the disk, it is recommended to illuminate with a light with a white spectrum like a neon around 9500°K.

<u>What to Do Once the Seeds Germinate?</u>

First, you need to make sure the roots have come out of the jiffy.

Take the jiffy (trying not to touch the plant or the roots with your hands) and place it in the pot with the earth or coconut fiber.

You can continue to water with the solution containing the root stimulator.

Chapter 4.
TOP HACK BEST ENVIRONMENT HOW-TOs

In order to germinate, the seed needs heat, water, oxygen, and soil that allows the coleoptile (grasses) or cup (legumes and dicotyledons in general) to reach sunlight in a short time (approximately a few days).

The actual germination phase, on the other hand, does not require light because the energy and matter needed to cover the needs of initial development are provided by the nutritional reserves accumulated in the seed itself.

There are, however, species with seeds characterized by positive photosensitivity, i.e., which start germination only after having received a specific dose of light, or negative, i.e., in total absence.

However, the light does not hinder the germination of the majority of our crops, so much so that the burial, from this point of view, is often superfluous. On the other hand, a good covering is required to guarantee the seed's constant conditions of temperature and humidity during germination.

The temperature requirements are different from species to species. For those grown in temperate climates, the ideal temperatures are generally between 18 and 24°C. Among the autumn-sown species, some, such as barley and soft wheat, manage to germinate even with temperatures a few degrees above zero. Spring-sown species (especially if of tropical or sub-tropical origin, such as soybeans and beans) are much more demanding in terms of temperature. Maize, apart from the wide genetic variability, requires at least 12 °C to provide regular and relatively rapid germination.

The soil temperature is especially important for spring sowing because it is a cold season, and the species are more demanding. To 'warm up the land, you need to work it. A worked soil, even only on the surface, tends to heat up sooner because the tillage reduces the presence of residue, which, by covering the surface, slows down both evaporation and heating by radiation. In addition to this, the tillage favors the evaporation of water: dry soil has a lower thermal inertia and therefore heats up sooner than wet soil. Warm soil allows early spring sowing.

For the germination process to begin and be completed, the water in the soil that surrounds the seed must be sufficient to imbibe its integuments and reach the embryo; furthermore, it must be available in abundance during the entire process, at least until the first roots develop. In fact, unlike the seed, which absorbs water by mere pressure difference, the roots are able to drink water even with active mechanisms.

The third factor of germination is the oxygen that must be available in the soil. In fact, with the rupture of the protective integument induced by the absorption of water, the oxygen penetrates inside the seed allowing the germination metabolism to proceed with the mobilization of the reserve substances (and supply energy through the aerobic Krebs cycle) and the synthesis of proteins and other substances required by development.

Finally, the soil must have a structure such to allow the protrusion of the radicle and the growth of the organ, which, coming out of the soil, will give rise to the first leaves (this organ is called hypocotyl when the cotyledons emerge from the earth; epicotyl when the cotyledons remain within the ground). It is, therefore, important that the developing seedling has the possibility of reaching the atmosphere before running out of nutrient reserves. With the exit of the cup from the soil, photosynthesis can begin, and with it, the liberation from the nutritional funds of the seed: the progressive and balanced development of leaves and roots will allow the plant to progress in its growth.

Lighting and Temperature

Like water, lighting is essential for a plant. In a mature plant, light allows the plant to form sugars from water and carbon dioxide. The plant then uses those sugars to fuel its growth, something we humans call photosynthesis.

For a germinated seed, lighting is also essential as long as it provides warmth, which a seed needs at the beginning to spread its shell and send its root into the soil. The best way to provide your seeds with the temperature they need is with fluorescent lights. (color temperature of 6500°K).

Fluorescent lights are ideal because they don't consume too much energy and don't give off too much heat.

You can put them as close to a young plant as possible, and while your seedling doesn't need them at that moment, it will as soon as those first few leaves start poking through the top of the soil.

You can't use them for growing, but for germination, they work fine. You can also use a heating mat, this heats the seeds from the bottom instead of the top, and you can use it even in the first stage of the germinated seed.

Keep the soil temperature around 24°. Seeds germinate best in humid, warm temperatures, similar to spring. To create this favorable environment, wrap plastic around your pot. Just make sure to remove the wrap the moment you see the sprouts appearing out of the ground. If the soil, water, or anything else you are growing in is hotter than 24°C, move the lamp away from the plant. Dry air won't kill the seedlings, but if you can reduce it, even better.

Where to Germinate Seeds

When you plan your outdoor cultivation, and you have received your seeds, it is best to germinate them indoors. That's because it's much easier to keep the correct temperature, water levels, and light exposure indoors. Even if you plan to grow your plants outdoors, you shouldn't try to start them outdoors (unless absolutely necessary). Outside you have to worry about rain, clouds, and many other things that could prevent your seeds from germinating. You'll also need to wait until the final frost has passed, which means your growing season may be delayed compared to if you started the seeds indoors. Starting indoors gives you an edge and your plants a better chance of survival.

If you still intend to germinate outdoors, choose a location that will support the plant throughout its life. You won't move the plant, so choose wisely. Plant the seeds when corn is usually planted in your area. Dig 6x6x6 holes at least 1 meter apart from one another and fill them with potting soil.

This will provide the seeds with enough nutrients to get started.

Next, dig a small hole a quarter-inch deep in the potting soil and drop the seed. Soak that soil with water and refill it again in a few days if the climate condition is warm enough. You can use greenhouses to protect your seeds to keep the area warm; still, be careful not to leave them on for too long – young plants will need light once they break through the ground.

There is, of course, an advantage to starting seeds outdoors if you plan to grow them there: your plant will have more time to adjust to the surrounding environment and will be less likely to suffer shock when moved outdoors. So, know what you're doing: remember to leave plenty of room for your plants (those tiny seeds can expand quite large), see the weather conditions in your environment, keep an eye out for animals that might eat your seeds, and use potting soil to provide just the right amount. of nutrients.

Plant your Germinated Seeds

Once your seeds have germinated, they should be planted. If you have been using a germination method that requires you to move the shoots, do it carefully, as the taproot is very fragile. You don't have to touch it. If you break it, although it may survive, it will definitely stunt your plant's growth.

When planting, drop the white root downwards. It should be placed about 3-5cm into the growing medium (up to the knuckles). The top of the seed, on the other hand, should be just below the surface.

Cover lightly and wait for the seedling to break through the soil for about a week (9-10 days maximum). It could emerge the same day, but if it hasn't appeared within ten days, it probably hasn't survived.

If your seed is accidentally planted upside down, don't worry. Nature has a way of working on its own. As long as there is enough space for the roots to grow, eventually, they will. Give it some time, and let it do its job!

Germination doesn't have to be complicated. It all starts with the right seeds. Our high-quality seeds will enhance your germination efforts.

Chapter 5.
GERMINATING SUCCESSFULLY: 6 FINAL TRICKS

1. Choose the Most Suitable Method for Your Type of Cultivation

There are several techniques for germinating seeds: if you intend to use a hydroponics system, Rockwool or Root Riot cubes are the ideal choices. If you grow in soil or coconut fiber, you can use Jiffy disks and switch to a small pot with slightly fertilized soil.

2. Plant More Seeds Than Chosen

Not all seeds germinate, so it is advisable to put more seeds to germinate than those chosen in case some do not. If all the seeds planted germinate, you can keep them all (if you have the space) or choose the best plants to grow until harvest!

3. Pre-Soaking the Seeds

This is optional, but if you choose to soak the seeds for at least six hours and no more than 12, you can place the slightly hatched and 'softened' seed directly into the cube or directly into the potting soil. This step allows you to significantly speed up the seed-hatching process by at least two days and to further select the seeds.

The water must be at room temperature, and very small doses of stimulators can be added to promote germination.

4. Keep Humidity and Temperature Constant

There are many propagators to choose from, each suited to a different environment. For winter weather, a heated propagator may be the best choice; this helps to achieve the necessary temperature and humidity. For the hot climate, unheated plastic greenhouses can also be used. It is highly recommended to nebulize the water in the internal part of the propagator; this favors the right humidity level.

5. Correct Lighting

To facilitate the germination process of the seeds, it is advisable to use lights with a cold-blue color spectrum, such as CFL bulbs or neon tubes. These lamps produce little heat and can be placed near plants to maximize the light they receive.

6. Have Patience!

Don't try to transplant plants too soon. Some seeds show signs of growth in less than 24 hours; others can take 3-4 days or more just to get out of the cube. It can be tempting to transplant as soon as the plants unfurl their first leaves, but the wait will pay off for the grower!

Maintaining high humidity (80-100%) and stable temperatures between 21°C and 26°C, your seedlings will be ready for potting after 10-28 days (depending on the seed). In 10-28 days, most plants have developed a strong root system and are ready to start the vegetative growth phase.

Chapter 6.
USEFUL ACCESSORIES FOR INDOOR SEED GERMINATION

The right accessories help your seeds grow into seedlings. You can find them in our indoor cultivation equipment shop: I will also give you valuable advice and answers to all your doubts!

Germination Jars

Seedbeds and germination pots are particularly suitable for seed development in indoor cultivation. The pots keep the sprouts separate, preventing the roots from intertwining; this way, you can prevent the growth of one seedling from damaging the others.

Make sure the jars are clean and have holes for water to drain.

Germination Lamps

Germination lamps produce a very bright spectrum of light, giving the sprout the light it needs to develop.

At the beginning of their life, the seedlings will need fluorescent or CFL, MH, and CMH grow lights.

Be careful, though: excessive lighting during the first few weeks can be harmful. After two weeks of exposure to these lights, you can start using high-pressure sodium (HPS with Agro spectrum) lamps.

Rooting by Seeds

To help your seeds germinate, you can use a rooting agent for seeds, which stimulates and strengthens the roots' growth, ensuring the plant's healthy and vigorous development.

They are essential for the root system of plants, but not only: they help prevent diseases and attacks by potentially dangerous parasites.

Storage of Unused Seeds

Proper seed storage, both before germination indoors and for unplanted seeds, is critical to growing sprouts.

Keep them in a cool and dry place with no excessive temperature range between the summer and autumn periods. Well-preserved seeds can last for many years.

You can also preserve them in the fridge at a temperature of 4°/5°C.

Pro Tip: Most seed savers use a cataloged storing system. Here's how it's structured:

a plastic container with an airtight seal, preferably in the shape of a briefcase, so that you can carry it with you comfortably;

Mini containers of the same condition as the mother container, in such a way as to each contain a different type of seed.

So what do you get? A briefcase with, inside, plastic boxes with each one a different type of seed that you want to keep. Logically, before storing them in these boxes, remember to follow all the cleaning and drying procedures so they can then be stored in a dry, cool place.

Don't forget to attach a label with the name of the seed to each mini container, and buy several maxi containers to increase your seed bank!

Why Didn't My Seeds Germinate?

It may happen that some seeds do not germinate: it is a problem many seed savers may face in their first experiences. Don't worry: try to understand the causes so as not to make a mistake next time. The reasons for this unsuccessful attempt are several. Let's formulate some hypotheses:

- Too hot/cold temperatures are risky for the seed, which cannot germinate properly. Always maintain a stable temperature and measure it constantly;

- Too wet/dry: the ideal humidity is high, but the seed must not get too wet, or it will rot. Arid weather also damages the seed;

- The seed is poorly stored: pay attention to the origin of your seeds, and check that they have been well kept;

- Unique treatments needed: your semen may need special treatments, for example soaking for a few hours.

Test and understand what your seeds need and how to help them germinate!

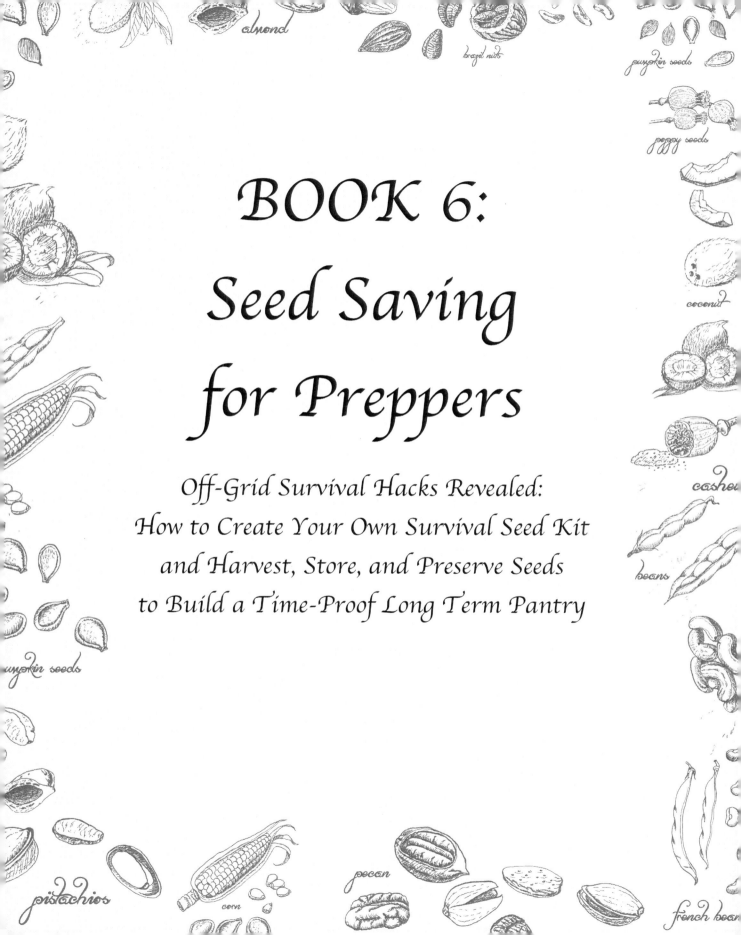

BOOK 6:
Seed Saving
for Preppers

Off-Grid Survival Hacks Revealed:
How to Create Your Own Survival Seed Kit
and Harvest, Store, and Preserve Seeds
to Build a Time-Proof Long Term Pantry

Chapter 1.
FROM SEED VAULT TO SEED VALUE

The famous Mayan prediction (or at least a popular interpretation) fortunately didn't turn out right. But fears of an end to the world or the occurrence of major natural disasters remain in many of us, like the fear of starving.

No danger, though: a magic jar has been devised in the United States that could guarantee precious reserves.

Seed Vault contains a kit of 20 essential seeds varieties, which can produce healthy food in extreme emergencies. Crops grown from these seeds are fast-growing and capable of feeding a large family. Each packet of seeds is vacuum sealed to ensure longer shelf life than canned foods or other preserved foods. The seeds are not genetically modified and are open-pollinated to increase the likelihood that they will develop once planted.

During the 2015 Expo, which was held in Milan in the Switzerland pavilion, you could find four towers full of food, the beginning of a social experiment that put a strain on the voracity of visitors.

In front of food, it is difficult to hold back. Still, at the basis of the social experiment, there was precisely the intention of understanding how people would behave in the face of limited resources. With this awareness and the question-title 'Is that for everyone?' every patron was aware that, once the four floors were finished, the resources of water, coffee, apples, and salt would not be refilled.

Our planet is in the same place as the tower floors during the first weeks of the experiment: on the verge of collapse. Here, another piece is added, derived from Alfred Henry Lewis's statement in 1906: 'nine meals from anarchy.' The argument, also attributed to Lord Cameron of Dillington, was taken up in 2008 by the Daily Mail with the onset of the economic crisis. Imagine that food resources are visibly limited, i.e., supermarket shelves are now empty (Venezuela in 2016, for example); how long would it take you to rob your neighbor or commit other crimes to be sure you will have a meal to eat? Nine meals. Then anarchy, loss of control, and pure indomitable survival instinct.

The scenario is apocalyptic, and leaving aside conspiracy theories about governments, this is where the preppers come into play. Thinking of a similar scenario: probably many of us would not be prepared to face it from many points of view.

One (better said, many) question arises: how many of us have food supplies in preparation for an irreparable crisis or a zombie invasion? And how many of us have solid first-aid knowledge?

We can address the argument ironically or realistically; preppers do it concretely and also out of passion. They are in charge of preparing for any type of emergency, ranging from the financial crisis to the atomic bomb. These groups of people train to respond to medical emergencies and lack of electricity, water, or food. They can be confused with survivalists who, except for subtle differences, deal with more or less the same issues with a more military style. The construction of shelters, the preparation of food and medicine supplies, and tools capable of providing energy are some of the requirements necessary to be part of the category. For those who have made even small stocks because of worse times, one could say they are already a bit of a prepper.

Among the solutions in case of significant emergencies is the relatively safer one of remaining locked up inside the house, even better if one has thought of building an ad hoc shelter. Bugging in, in the jargon, is a practice diametrically opposed to bugging out, which instead requires you to leave your home taking all the necessary tools with you.

In a similar situation, nothing is left to chance. Regarding food, the situation changes according to the type of emergency, and in this context, army rations can undoubtedly prove to be functional.

Vegetable seeds are extremely precious goods, such as long-life foods, and therefore all canned ones. The FIFO rule applies: first, in-first out, what is kept first must be consumed before all the rest. It takes rigor and order, mental and practical, both of which are difficult to maintain if the whole world is in chaos.

Among the foods adopted by the preppers is the pemmican, a preparation that, at first glance, has the appearance of a futuristic dish, usually prepared with dried meat powder mixed with fat and spices. It is a food which, due to its nutritional values, has proved to be very useful in polar expeditions, and for preppers, it has proved to be ideal precisely because it can be held for a long time, it is caloric, and very nutritious.

The original recipe comes from Native Americans, but in the event of nuclear war, a supply of MRE is also recommended: meal-ready-to-eat. These are the well-known K rations used by the army, which also exist in a civilian version and can be found on the market. Each allocation guarantees three daily meals; the American and the Italian ones have become the most famous because they are considered the best. Indeed, these are not gourmet preparations, but the rations are optimal for mobile units that have to move for short periods and are a resource that also attracts preppers a lot. Furthermore, pemmican remains one of the favorite foods because it was found in an excellent state of conservation and possibly edible even after over twenty years.

Governments, economic crises, threats of nuclear wars, but also a large part of the post-apocalyptic narrative in the style of 'I am legend,' without counting the films of the same genre and/or catastrophic (Roland Emmerich is a master at this) and the TV series, which can be found in a "The Walking Dead" or a lighter and more carefree version such as "The last man on Earth."

Watching or reading something belonging to the vein, surely we have all wondered how we would behave; well, preppers take care of answering the question if that could happen.

In this scenario, it goes without saying, how the seeds and their rescue represent an immeasurable added value if one of the apocalyptic scenarios described above occurs. In a rush of Darwinian memory, only the prepared ones and those who know how to give life - literally - to food that can be consumed, even in desperate conditions, will be able to save themselves on this earth.

And the seeds, therefore, symbolise precisely the promise of a new life that can be reborn, thanks to our taking care of them.

In this Book, therefore, we will deal exactly with how preppers interpret and implement harvesting, germinating, and seed saving. We're going to reveal what the hacks are to preserve them in an off-grid situation and, of course, how to create your own seed survival kit to build a time-proof long-term pantry.

Let's go!

Chapter 2.
EMERGENCY SEED KIT: INITIAL TIPS

Climate change, political turmoil, and habitat losses cause some of us to turn to survival-planning thoughts. You don't have to become a conspiracy theorist or a hermit to know how to save and plan for an emergency kit. For gardeners, storing survival seeds is a future source of food in dire need and an excellent way to perpetuate and preserve a favorite heirloom plant.

Heirloom Emergency Survival Seeds need to be adequately prepared and stored for any specific use down the line. Here are my tips on how to create a prepper's survival seed vault.

<u>What is a Survival Seed Vault?</u>

Survival Seed Vault Storage is more than just creating future crops. Survival seed preservation is done by the USA Department of Agriculture and other national organizations worldwide. What is a Survival Seed Vault? It's a way to preserve seeds not only for next season's crops but also for future needs.

Survival seeds are organic, heirloom, and cross-pollinated (we addressed this topic vastly in Book 4 of this Collection). An emergency seed stock should avoid GMO and hybrid seeds, which don't produce good seeds, can contain harmful toxins and are generally sterile. Sterile plants of these seeds are of little use in a perpetual survival garden and require the constant purchase of seeds from companies that hold patents on the modified crop.

Of course, the safe harvesting of seeds is of little value without carefully managing the storage of survival seeds. Also, you should keep the seeds that will produce the food you will eat and will grow well in every climate, especially your environment.

Emergency Survival Seed Supply Tips

- The internet is an excellent way to source secure seeds for storage. There are many organic and pollinated sites open, as well as seed exchange forums. If you're already an avid gardener, saving seeds starts with helping some of yours to flower and seed or saving fruit and harvesting the seed.

- Choose only plants that thrive in most conditions and are heirlooms. Your emergency seed vault should have enough seeds to grow next year's crop and still have some remaining seeds.

- Careful seed rotation will help ensure that the freshest seed is saved while the aging ones are planted first. This way, you will always have the seed ready if you want a second sowing in the season or a crop fails. Consistent food is the goal and can easily be achieved if the seeds are stored correctly.

- As we saw in Book 1, the Svalbard Global Seed Vault in Norway has more than 740,000 seed samples. And that is excellent news but hardly helpful for those of us in North America, as Norway is a perfect place to store seeds due to its cold climate.

- As we already pointed out, we should store seeds in a dry place where the temperature is 40 degrees Fahrenheit (4 C.) or lower.

- We should also use moisture-proof containers and avoid exposing the seeds to light. If you're harvesting your seed, hang it out to dry before placing it in a container.

- Some seeds, such as tomatoes, must be soaked for a few days to remove the pulp. This is where a very fine sieve comes in handy. Once you have separated the seeds from the juice and pulp, dry them the same way you do the seeds and then place them in the containers.

Label all the plants in your survival seed vault and date them. Rotate seeds as they are used to ensure the best germination and freshness.

Chapter 3.
PREPARING FOOD FOR THE NEXT CRISIS

Is preparing for a food crisis really possible? As we have seen in the scenarios listed above, it is not always easy to standardize the strategies to be put into practice because situations can vary greatly depending on the event triggering the food crisis.

In general, however, we can immediately learn and put into practice valuable strategies much loved by preppers or at least gain more awareness on the subject.

As you've probably learned elsewhere, grocery stores have about three days' worth of stock — when the trigger event occurs, people will rush in and buy as much as possible. The food will likely vanish in high-density areas in less than a day or hours.

If something were to put the food supply chain in danger for a long time, there would be violence and chaos in most communities. It is very important to start thinking about it NOW and get used to asking ourselves questions.

Since the Covid19 began to spread throughout the world and in our state, causing generalized lockdowns, amidst the various thoughts of seclusion malaise, I could not help but think: 'It could have been worse, much worse. What would have happened in my country?" The whole world as we know it could have changed in a few days, dragging the population into absolute chaos.

There are several ways to start approaching the topic. Since we may not always know what to prepare for, it is useful to prepare for any scenario, even for long periods.

1. Create Food Supplies

You should view your prepper pantry as a long-term investment. One of the best prepper's communities' advice (and mine too) is to buy food that you really like to eat: it's preliminary advice that can contribute to saving lives. If a major SHTF event does not occur on your food's expiration date, you will always be able to eat it without disgust (without spending additional money on food) and thus renew your supplies.

One of the first problems you will face in approaching stocking is choosing the way to store food properly. You may need to dedicate some space in your home to store excess food, whether frozen, dried, or canned. It could mean buying an extra freezer or some closed shelves.

If you have an unused room or maybe a basement, you can start stockpiling there. If you live in a condominium and have a basement space, always pay attention to what others might see.

Remember that you should have easy access to this room and that very few people should know about its existence.

Always check the storage recommendations (for example, temperature and humidity) on the packages and verify that they correspond to those of the room in which you will start storing.

Decide what food you want to keep and how much. This depends on the period of the food crisis and, of course, on the budget you intend to invest.

Before you start, list everything you like, and consider that your basket should contain a good mix of vitamins, carbohydrates, minerals, fats, and proteins. In a food crisis, the most vital food will be the one with the most carbohydrates, the main fuel for physical energy and also a higher mood. So keep in mind that you must have products such as rice, pasta, and cereals.

2. Make Your Own Food

Here we are. While stocking up on food is very important, in a long-term food crisis, it may be wiser to have built the means to produce your own food.

The supply will be the stop-gap needed to feed you as new fresh food grows. A master seed saver knows how to do it. Here are two ways to start being auto-sufficient.

a) Cultivate the Land and Raise Crops

If you live in a city and do not have a backyard, you should consider buying at least one plot in the countryside. As is often the case, most of the victims of famine are citizens. The war stories of my grandmother ('poor in the money but rich in fields' in Montana) and my grandfather are decidedly distant. My grandmother never suffered from hunger during her childhood, and in her rural area, everyone was engaged in the production of vegetables, meat, or vegetables: of course, this does not mean that now and then, some troops did not pass by to raid. To date, it is difficult to standardize the effects of war on a territory: we do not know what could happen.

Living in the countryside usually makes it much easier to get food and overcome a food crisis. If you don't know much about gardening, start small with a few garden boxes for herbs, tomatoes, or sprouts. Start preparing early on seed production - they'll be harder to find later.

You can also raise animals. Start with pets that can provide you with something extra: hens for eggs, cows or sheep for milk, fish for fish eggs. Just like stocking up on food, think that you should be getting all the vitamins, carbohydrates, proteins, fats, and minerals.

Remember that you may need to:

- Protect your crop from looters: mark your land in a visible way and, if you have the means, try building a fenced yard. Somehow it will make things more difficult for the bad guys. Furthermore, a plot not too far from home will be preferable to a larger one further away;

- Learn about food storage: You may need to store food for the winter or build a food supply just in case. Food preservation comes in many forms: dehydrating, freezing, vacuum packing… Some tools and materials are needed, along with a good deal of knowledge. They are an investment of time and money you won't regret;

- Storing the seeds: as we anticipated in the previous paragraph, find out about the methods for collecting the seeds to plant them the following year. Collect your seeds from the healthiest plants. Each plant has its own methods: try to prepare yourself in advance;

- Exchange food to replenish other materials that you cannot obtain otherwise.

Some interesting books can come in handy if you still have some gaps in the moment of SHTF, other than this one: study, study, study!

However, we advise you to practice right away, even with a small vegetable garden on the balcony: you have no idea what it will teach you.

b) Grow Indoors

For emergencies, small spaces, or periods when producing fresh vegetables is not possible, remember systems such as microgreens and aquaponics.

Microgreens, 'young' plants rich in nutrients, are considered a superfood. They are very rich in nutrients and, for the same weight as the same grown vegetable, they have a higher level of vitamins and bioactive substances. We are discussing the topic of microgreens in the next paragraph.

Later we will also explore the theme of aquaponics (in particular, the 'hydroponic' variant) for indoor crops, so don't miss it. This system provides you with all kinds of vegetables and saves you up to 90% of water because it recirculates within the system instead of filtering: not bad in the case of SHTF!

Plus, plants grow faster: plants are always getting new nutrients, so you'll need half the space compared to gardening in soil.

Chapter 4.
HOW-TO STRATEGIES

Climate change, political turmoil, and habitat losses cause some of us to turn to survival-planning thoughts. You don't have to become a conspiracy theorist or a hermit to know how to save and plan for an emergency kit. For gardeners, storing survival seeds is a future source of food in dire need and an excellent way to perpetuate and preserve a favorite heirloom plant.

Heirloom Emergency Survival Seeds need to be adequately prepared and stored for any specific use down the line. Here are my tips on how to create a prepper's survival seed vault.

What is a Survival Seed Vault?

Survival Seed Vault Storage is more than just creating future crops. Survival seed preservation is done by the USA Department of Agriculture and other national organizations worldwide. What is a Survival Seed Vault? It's a way to preserve seeds not only for next season's crops but also for future needs.

Survival seeds are organic, heirloom, and cross-pollinated (we addressed this topic vastly in Book 4 of this Collection). An emergency seed stock should avoid GMO and hybrid seeds, which don't produce good seeds, can contain harmful toxins and are generally sterile. Sterile plants of these seeds are of little use in a perpetual survival garden and require the constant purchase of seeds from companies that hold patents on the modified crop.

Of course, the safe harvesting of seeds is of little value without carefully managing the storage of survival seeds. Also, you should keep the seeds that will produce the food you will eat and will grow well in every climate, especially your environment.

Emergency Survival Seed Supply Tips

- The internet is an excellent way to source secure seeds for storage. There are many organic and pollinated sites open, as well as seed exchange forums. If you're already an avid gardener, saving seeds starts with helping some of yours to flower and seed or saving fruit and harvesting the seed.

- Choose only plants that thrive in most conditions and are heirlooms. Your emergency seed vault should have enough seeds to grow next year's crop and still have some remaining seeds.

- Careful seed rotation will help ensure that the freshest seed is saved while the aging ones are planted first. This way, you will always have the seed ready if you want a second sowing in the season or a crop fails. Consistent food is the goal and can easily be achieved if the seeds are stored correctly.

- As we saw in Book 1, the Svalbard Global Seed Vault in Norway has more than 740,000 seed samples. And that is excellent news but hardly helpful for those of us in North America, as Norway is a perfect place to store seeds due to its cold climate.

- As we already pointed out, we should store seeds in a dry place where the temperature is 40 degrees Fahrenheit (4 C.) or lower.

- We should also use moisture-proof containers and avoid exposing the seeds to light. If you're harvesting your seed, hang it out to dry before placing it in a container.

- Some seeds, such as tomatoes, must be soaked for a few days to remove the pulp. This is where a very fine sieve comes in handy. Once you have separated the seeds from the juice and pulp, dry them the same way you do the seeds and then place them in the containers.

- Label all the plants in your survival seed vault and date them. Rotate seeds as they are used to ensure the best germination and freshness.

Chapter 5.
GROWING MICROGREENS

As we have said, these micro vegetables are superfoods, as they maintain very important nutritional elements for health. At the same weight compared to the large plant, therefore, microgreens have many more of these substances, even vitamins, and substances that are lost in the plant once it matures. For this reason, this technique is also adored by seed savers who also take care to embrace the prepper philosophy and start creating their own indoor garden.

Let's recall all the amazing properties of microgreens:

- They are easy to grow: usually, you don't even need to use pesticides to grow them because there are no parasites that need to be eliminated to protect microgreens;

- Growth time varies from 4 to 21 days, so you don't have to wait long to consume them;

- They don't need a lot of space to be produced, as a few shelves at home are enough!

- They are a valid and quality alternative for the prepper. A microgreen is easily produced from sprouts and ensures clean and healthy nutrition. Also, with microgreens, the food is fresh, which is not bad in a scenario where the foods we consume are mostly powdered, dried, or canned.

And remember: once cut, the plant dies. Therefore the prepper will have to count on a considerable supply of seeds to be able to feed on microgreens too. In addition, for cultivation, they need LED lights and air to caress the buds. However, in the case of bugging in during an emergency situation, being able to rely on a plant for the production of microgreens is a plus for the professional prepper.

So, what does it take to grow microgreens?

<u>Soil and Containers</u>

Microgreens need mixed soil, which is so rich in nutrients and has good water-holding capacity. To facilitate the choice, it is good to say that good soil must have these characteristics:

- Porosity over 85%: valid both for water retention and for a high level of aeration of the root system;
- The pH must be between 5.5 and 6.5;
- No heavy metals or pollutants.

For indoor cultivation of microgreens, you should use plastic containers such as tubs or trays. The dimensions are free to choose from, but it is advisable never to exceed 5 cm in height. In this way, the roots of the young plants will find water easily, and the seedlings will be adequately exposed to light.

Ensure that the bottom of the containers is perforated to avoid water stagnation which can compromise the quality of the microgreens.

<u>Lighting</u>

To give light to your microgreens, the use of LED lamps is strongly recommended as they do not produce heat, have an optimized spectrum to stimulate chlorophyll synthesis, and consume less energy than HPS or CFL lamps.

After germination in the dark, the microgreens must be placed under a lamp to receive light to grow well, which must be from 12 to 14 hours of light a day. For greater savings, we advise you to use LED lamps for cultivation; thanks to the use of brand-new LEDs, they are able to emit light very similar to that of the sun, with all the colors necessary for the development of the plant, infrared and ultraviolet included.

<u>Growing Microgreens</u>

To start your cultivation, you will have to wash the seeds under running water and start the 'pre-treatment phase.' You must therefore immerse the seeds in water to induce germination for a time that varies according to the type of seed. At this point, take your container, which you must fill, leaving 1 cm away from the edge, and proceed with sowing.

You must distribute the seeds uniformly on the surface: it is advisable to arrange them with a density of 1/4 seeds per cm². With a spray bottle, you must moisten them immediately to guarantee water for 2-3 days. At this point, cover the container with cling film (e.g., kitchen film) and leave them in the dark for 2-3 days. This stimulates germination, which must take place at a temperature between 20-24°, which becomes 16-18° in the growth phase.

Irrigation

If during germination, it is advisable to use nebulizers, when the seedlings have emerged from the earth, it is best to irrigate from below, thus acting on the substrate. Therefore, it becomes useful not to wet the young shoots or the leaves but to keep the soil moist.

Harvesting

The cultivation cycle of microgreens varies according to the species chosen, but generally, it can last from 5 to 21 days after germination, which varies from 2 to 5 days.

When the first true leaves appear, it is possible to proceed with the harvest. You can harvest your vegetables manually, cutting the seedlings a few millimeters from the surface. Your microgreens can then be stored for one or two weeks or cut to be eaten immediately.

Chapter 6.
HYDROPONIC SEEDS

Hydroponics is cultivating plants out of the soil, i.e., without soil. The roots are then immersed in water, where nutrients essential for luxuriant growth are dissolved. So, in hydroponic systems, the roots of the plant are immersed directly in the water, where nutrients are regularly dissolved. On the contrary, the vase is filled with an inert substrate, such as clay or perlite, in semi-hydroponic systems. We then proceed by marking the water level (about two fingers) and fertilizing regularly.

There are pots on the market that can facilitate semi-hydroponic cultivation and prevent the formation of algae and parasites. However, you need to pay attention to the water level to prevent your plants from suffering too much thirst or, on the contrary, the roots rot when they come into contact with the water.

What are the Most Suitable Plants for Hydroponic or Semi-Hydroponic Cultivation?

The plants most appreciate this type of cultivation are tropical plants, which often do not find the right degree of humidity in our apartments. By being immersed in the inert substrate, which is gradually moistened, the plant can enjoy constant humidity. However, some species of plants are particularly appreciated and suitable for hydroponic cultivation due to their characteristics: Lettuce. Tomatoes. Pepper, three of the plants and seeds we will discover, is part of the seed saver prepper kit!

What are the Advantages and Disadvantages?

Small and compact with a tank capacity of 1 liter. It can also be used wirelessly. Very quiet and equipped with a digital screen with a battery autonomy level.

The main advantages are:

- The greater possibility of controlling the development of the plant and, in particular, of its root system;
- the plant can autonomously manage its water needs, and therefore, the risk of overwatering or, on the contrary, making your plant go thirsty is reduced;
- plants grown in hydroponics or semi-hydroponics usually grow faster.

The disadvantages are:

- If you choose to use specific pots, the costs increase;
- if, instead, you choose to use glass pots, the risk is that algae form as the roots and the substrate are exposed to light;
- it is necessary to remember to enrich the cultivation water with adequate fertilizer, preferably slow release.

What Are the Materials for Semi-Hydroponic Cultivation?

If you choose to experiment with a semi-hydro system, these are the steps you will need to follow and the materials you will need:

- get yourself a vase or glass jar if you opt for a more homely system, otherwise choose from the many specific vases on the market;
- choose the inert substrate: expanded clay, perlite, or those already enriched with nutrients (lechuza pon, the mineral plant substrate);
- fill your vase with two fingers of the inert substrate and mark the water level on the vase; you can also choose two different types of inert to make checking the water level easier;
- clean the roots of your plant carefully - be careful to remove as much soil as possible to prevent mold from forming;
- insert your plant in the pot and fill it with the inert substrate.

Chapter 7.
YOUR SURVIVAL GARDEN

As we said earlier, no one can tell if the economic situation in the country will deteriorate to the point that you and your family will need a survival garden to survive. However, like putting together plans in the event of an earthquake or other disaster, the key to survival is preparation.

What is a Survival Garden?

A small garden with few plants to feed your entire family if all you would need to eat were the crops you grew.

Calculate the calories your family would need each day in order to survive well in a disaster situation, then see if you can name plants that can supply the fats, carbohydrates, and vitamins needed to keep you healthy.

With the global situation and the preppers communities spreading, survival family gardens have become a hot gardening trend. If you'll ever find yourself in an emergency situation that requires you to consume only garden crops, you'll be much better off if you learn something about the survival garden as well in advance of the need.

<u>Survival Garden How Tos</u>

How do you start designing survival family garden?

Start by working a small plot of land and learning on the job. You can even use containers if needed. The most important thing is to start practicing growing crops.

Start small in your garden with a few vegetables you enjoy eating.

You might try easy-to-grow vegetables like:

- Peas;
- Bush beans;
- Carrots;
- Potatoes.

Use open-pollinated seeds, such as heirloom seeds, as they will continue to produce.

As time passes and you become more familiar with gardening, consider which crops can give you the most calories for the space and remember to store them well. Practice growing them.

Calorie-rich crops include:

- Potatoes;
- Winter squash;
- Corn;
- Beans;
- Sunflower seeds.

Read survival gardening tips; read this book more than once. Look for crops that meet the nutritional needs that you can grow where you live (we will talk about it in the next paragraph.)

Remember that preserving your crops is as important as growing them, since you'll need to make the garden's riches last through the winter.

Vegetables that keep well include:

- Beetroots;
- Turnips;
- Carrots;
- Cabbage;
- Rutabagas (swedes);
- Onions;

- Leeks.

You can also dry, freeze and preserve many vegetable crops.

The more you keep practising growing these types of vegetables, the more prepared you will be to make a living off the land if and when the need arises.

Chapter 8.
PREPPER SURVIVAL SEED KIT

Before closing this Book dedicated to building a self-sufficient seed pantry in perfect prepper style, here's what you don't want to forget to build your emergency seed kit to always keep with you just in case. Scroll back through the pages of this Collection and restart the conservation of each seed and also of each variety of plants in order to begin to give life to your personalized kit.

First, however, some advice is not to be underestimated before starting to collect.

- Find out what functions best in your area and when to plant for.

- Calculate how much space you have for growing and if it is adequate for feeding your family or group.

- Ask yourself: how many plants or varieties do I need to sustain my family?

- Start with easier varieties: stock up on all of the food varieties that you eat but it might be a great idea to plant the easiest ones:

  1. Swiss Chard;

2. Radish;

3. Lettuce;

4. Green Beans;

5. Carrots;

6. Cucumber;

7. Zucchini;

8. Tomato;

9. Beets.

Timing is everything: if you live in a very hot climate area, usually summer is not the best time to plant. If your zone is a cold one, it is best to plant indoors or provide a greenhouse to extend your growing season.Learn to save your seeds: that's what we are doing, right? :)

All the seeds to build your own kit:

• Beans;

• Spinach;

• Squash;

• Allium varieties - onions, shallots, leeks, and garlic;

• Broccoli;

• Peppers;

• Eggplant;

• Asparagus;

• Amaranth;

• Corn - among grains, corn deserves a specific mention. While it might not be the easiest crop to grow, it has many uses. Sweet corn, but also dent corn & field corn. They can be dried and fed to livestock;

• Grains.

Extras:

• Herbs: medicinal herbs are a must;

• Flowers: Borage, PurpleConeflower, Marigolds, Nasturtium, Plains Coreopsis, Cornflower, Yarrow, sunflowers, and Calendula - that can also generate their seeds;

• Potatoes: pretty easy to grow, although some varieties are very disease prone;

Edible seeds: sunflower, flax, chia, sesame, etc. For these seeds, you can also make an exception since they are easy to find and last many years if kept in excellent condition. Start stockpiling!

BOOK 7:
Make Money with Your Beloved Seeds

Learn how to Sell Excess Seeds,
Monetize Your Hard Work
and Make Infinite ROI

Chapter 1.
A MATTER OF RESISTANCE

Following an international legal battle, enthusiasts but also expert farmers who have grown and shared their seeds for thousands of years risk being judged as criminals. A few large corporations dominate three-quarters of the global seed market, which turns into every one of the commodities that dominate agribusiness.

Environmental activists and even seed savers are fighting to repeal unethical laws that deprive farmers of the right to store and exchange their seeds. Their argument is based on the notion that whoever controls our food supplies, in fact, controls the entire world, its functioning, and even its rescue (or non-rescue).

This leads to the loss of their autonomy and decision-making capacity for seed savers and farmers. They are forced to buy patented seeds from seed corporations, often hybrid and modified seeds.

An example is the 'terminator' seeds, genetically modified to become sterile after the first harvest. In addition to being very expensive, this typology requires large quantities of pesticides and artificial fertilizers, all products offered at a high price by the corporations themselves.

Consequently, year after year, farmers have to continue to buy seeds and pesticides. Those that are not swamped by debt, therefore, become part of the corporate production chain.

Agricultural biodiversity is essential to counter many of the challenges we face globally, as we have seen: the emergence of new types of diseases, the harmful effects of climate change, and socio-economic difficulties.

The adaptability of a certain type of crop has always been a very important element for our survival: yet, according to a study by the FAO, during the 20th century, agricultural biodiversity decreased by 75% following the privatization processes and the extensive use of monocultures (the uninterrupted cultivation of the same kind of plant in the same portion of land).

Here, then, becoming a seed saver can represent a resistance against the monopoly of seeds.

Many farmers continued to grow local seed varieties, risking fines and even imprisonment. They protested, went on strike, and refused to surrender. Sometimes they managed to win. Their successes, however small they may seem, have had an incredible impact on the individuals directly involved.

These farmers may not be able to change the world immediately, but their efforts will continue to change their society, which in turn will lead to global changes.

In the meantime, for all this to end, in the best possible way, with a recognition of the monumental work of seed savers to help the planet, here's how you can set up your profitable business without risking repercussions but, rather, maximizing your investment.

Chapter 2.
HOW TO SELL EXCESS SEEDS

In a curt answer: you can't! Following pressure from powerful multinationals in the agricultural sector, seed sharing has been banned in some American states, and even in Europe, the conditions for seed selling are almost invisible.

Still, there is a way to build a profitable business that revolves around this wonderful art... I'll tell you about it in a bit!

Sharing seeds is a practice as old as agriculture, a legacy of an era in which human life was inextricably linked to the earth. This practice is able to ensure the maintenance of biodiversity and local food security.

Seeds are not simply future plants; they contain primordial knowledge and needs; they are a collective good far from the logic of maximizing yield and profit that characterize patented seeds.

Yet the sharing of seeds, an activity that is not only harmless but beneficial for the territory, is considered illegal in several areas of the United States.

In some countries, permits are required for the sale of the seeds, which must also be correctly labeled and tested. The problem with these state laws is that they were thought and written to regulate the commercial seed industry, not small-community trading, which is penalized.

Surely you can give away packets of your grandmother's heirloom purple tomato seeds, right? Wrong! In most states, there are rules that require tests of germination paces and weed-seed percentages any time seeds switch hands.

This issue is a hurdle for homesteaders who might want to turn that unique mixture they saved or developed into a micro business.

A good tip is to search states' laws to match the Recommended Uniform State Seed Law (RUSSL), which allows seed libraries, swaps, and seed banks while still protecting the economic system that makes the production of new attainable varieties.

After all, the free sharing of seeds is so valuable that the US Patent office used to spend nearly a third of its budget mailing out packets to farmers. Who says your grandmother's heirloom tomato seeds aren't valuable?

That's why seed exchange and seed libraries, structures in which users, in addition to books, can borrow vegetable seeds which they will then return in spring by obtaining them from the harvest of their own gardens, are now an important tool for sharing and preserving ancient species and biodiversity.

Public access to seeds has declined since the 1980s when a Supreme Court ruling ruled that a form of life can be patented. This choice has favored the multinationals who have developed standardized 'uniform and stable' seeds created precisely to be repurchased as they are rapidly depleted and cannot be re-sown.

It is, therefore, evident how seed sharing and libraries are considered obstacles by powerful companies in the agricultural sector who claim a monopoly in seed management.

Banning and outlawing nature, because we are talking about seeds, is something so arrogant as to be almost hideous.

Let's see together how the seed savers are organized.

Chapter 3.
CREATE YOUR SEED LIBRARY

To put it simply, a seed library is what it sounds like: it lends seeds to gardeners and seed savers. It's easy, it is useful, and it's great for your business. It's a way to have fun, build community with other seed savers, and support gardeners and beginners.

Also, keep rare, open-pollinated, or heirloom seeds and encourage gardeners to keep quality seeds suitable for their local growing area.

So how does a seed library work? A seed library takes effort and dedication to put together, but its functioning is very catchy: gardeners 'borrow' or exchange seeds from the library when planting time comes.

When the growing season ends, they harvest the seeds from the plants and give back a portion of the seeds to the library.

If you have the funds, you can offer your library seed lending for free. If not, you may need to charge a small application fee to cover expenses.

How to Start a Seed Library

If you're interested in building your own seed library, here are a few things to consider before starting your journey!

- Present your ideas to a local group, such as a master gardener or club, and sees saving's network. There is a lot to do, so you will need a group of interested people.

- Set up a convenient space, such as a community building. Often, actual libraries are willing to dedicate space for a seed library. (They don't take up much space.)

- Gather your materials. You will need a wooden cabinet with dividable drawers, labels, seed bags, stamps, and stamps. Ask local hardware stores for sponsoring and support: garden centers or other local businesses may be willing to donate their materials.

- You will also need a seed database (or another system for keeping track of them). Free and open-source databases are also available online.

- Ask local gardeners for seed donations. Don't worry about having a large variety of seeds at the start. Starting small is a good idea. Late summer and fall (seed saving period) is the best time to request seeds.

- Decide the categories for your seeds. Many libraries use the classifications 'super easy', 'easy,' and 'hard' to describe the level of difficulty involved in planting, nurturing, and saving seeds.

- You will also want to divide the seeds by plant type (i.e., flowers, vegetables, herbs, etc., or perennials, annuals, or biennials).

- Include classifications for heirloom plants and native wildflowers.

- There are many possibilities, so devise a grading system that suits you and your borrowers.

- Set your own ground rules. For example, do you want all seeds to be grown organically? Are pesticides okay?

- Gather a group of volunteers. To begin with, you'll need people to run the library, sort and package the seeds, and create advertisements.

- You can promote your library by inviting professional or experienced gardeners to give informative presentations or seminars.

- Spread the word about your library with posters, flyers, and brochures. Be sure to provide seed saving information!

Pro Tip: at this point, your goal is to get yourself known and create 'noise' around you, your expertise, and the good you are doing for your local area and to help seed conservation as well. Including your brilliant plans for the near future.

Create a collection of useful contacts and numbers and offer your help and cooperation if needed. In short, let yourself be known!

In the next section, we'll look at how you can turn this mostly incomeless business into a profitable business that revolves around your personal brand.

Chapter 4.
YOUR BELOVED SEEDS WITH INFINITE ROI

Have you heard of affiliations, and would you like to try earning from affiliate links too? It is an excellent idea! Among the various marketing techniques, this is certainly the simplest one for those who do not want to invest money and have little technical skills, not to mention the impossibility of being able to sell the fruit of your hard work (the seeds, of course)!

However, even if you can't sell the seeds, you can make your seeds sell... you!

The success of your upcoming business depends on several factors: first of all, your reliability and the trust you have built (as shown in the previous chapter.) If you suggest something, it's because you've tried it or feel you can confidently promote it. The more people will take action on your recommendation and are satisfied with it, the stronger the bond of trust that binds you to them will be.

As a result, it will be much easier for you to continue promoting your products or services.

Let's find out how together.

Affiliate marketing is based on an agreement between a company that sells a service or product and an affiliate, person, or company that promotes it. For this promotion, the advertiser company pays a percentage or a sum on the conversion.

Generally, the conversion is the sale, i.e., the affiliate earns only if his promotion leads to a purchase, but this is not always the case.

The type of conversion depends on the type of affiliate program: it can be a click, a download, a lead acquisition, and so on.

It is a different marketing concept from classic advertising, as you don't pay for the advertising space itself but for the conversion, the result.

Seed saving, as we have already said, doesn't allow you to sell your seeds, but it doesn't say anything about selling all the products that 'revolve' around the seeds themselves!

How to Start Earning with Affiliate Marketing?

To make money with affiliations, you need very little. Here is a step-by-step guide.

- First, you need to create your online presence (considering that the offline one is already well established in your local circle and among the seed savers communities): choose the right channel for you between social media and personal website and start spreading the word about your expert seed saver knowledge.

The more you commit yourself to this phase, the more people will follow you, recognizing the value of what you spread, and the more users you will have to offer your services and links to the products you recommend.

- Second, you need to define an affiliate program to participate in, such as that of Amazon. But Amazon is not the only one: many companies need followed and competent people who 'sell' their products under a commission on the sale. Look for the best ones to collaborate with, also respecting the point of view of your target audience.

For example, given that seed savers are fighting the seed monopoly, it wouldn't make sense to offer a Monsanto product, don't you think?

- Create your 'own' house: your website. Can you make money with affiliate marketing without having a website? Is it possible to make money with affiliations without having a website? It depends. Although having an already-read and known blog or site can help you maximize your income, it is not mandatory, as recommended, to have your platform. However, many affiliate marketing platforms require it, also to guarantee your audience and your reliability. The site or blog must have been around for a certain period and must be up to date.

However, many influencers take advantage of affiliate links by working exclusively with social networks without relying on a site. For example, using a dedicated revenue system or influencer programs.

- What to sell: as mentioned in point 2, the choice of products is essential for building your reputation as an expert and maximizing conversions in the niche of your users, acquaintances, and followers.

Choose all those products connected to seed saving concerning: the choice of seeds; collection; germination; instruments; drying; various techniques; conservation; exchange, etc. And remember that there are seeds of various species...

Therefore, open your mind and think about everything that has served you over time to build your seed bank: they are the same products that the people who follow you, beginners but also advanced, need tremendously!

And who better than you to sell them one they know is reliable because you've tried it and used it yourself?

Working with Affiliates: How Much Can You Earn?

How do these affiliations work in practice? How do you earn from these programs? It's very simple. Once you have signed up for the system, you will receive an affiliate code or referral link. Anyone who performs an action via this link or using your code, for example, by purchasing a product or subscribing to a newsletter, will earn you the percentage or sum provided for by the program in question.

The personalized link traces the path that the user has taken and saves the crucial information: the visit and the purchase were generated thanks to your link.

There is an advantage on both sides: you will only have to promote the products, while affiliation companies will pay you after the sale. It's a win-win situation where everyone wins.

Yes, but how much do you earn? Amazon's program, for example, promises to earn you up to 12% in affiliate commissions for every sale you generate. But you can also reach different agreements with other companies, reaching much higher figures.

If your content is consistent with the links you offer, it won't be difficult for people to follow your advice. Of course, all of this must consider the type of commission envisaged within the program.

How-To Start:

- Choose a market niche

You need to choose a niche market that is suitable for selling affiliate products - this step is obvious for you! And, at this point, you should already be halfway there! If you haven't already done so, however, just read this book from scratch and apply its practical teachings ;)

- Create your site

You need to build the platform to publish your content and gain authority.

- Publish your first content

The contents will be the tool to generate traffic: show your skills and persuade you to buy. You are perfectly capable and competent.

- Request access to the affiliate programs of your interest

Once you have created the site and some content, the affiliate programs will be happy to welcome you.

- Enter affiliate links

Once you have access to the program, you just need to insert your affiliate links in the content.

- Take care of your Audience

No traffic = no users = no revenue. That's easy! If you really want to be successful in the affiliate marketing industry, you want to generate traffic through:

- Social media strategy/campaign;
- Valuable content and specialized tips for your niche;
- Advertising;
- Word of Mouth.

While focusing on these four points will earn you traffic, think harder with your affiliate work. You need to focus on your audience and your users.

Try to understand what value your suggestions can offer, which will be the key to capturing your audience, winning heavy traffic, and ultimately ensuring the success of your upcoming affiliate business while making infinite ROI!

CONCLUSION: IT'S UP TO YOU

What a journey we have made together! At this point, the art of saving seeds is no longer a secret for you: you have entered the network of world seed savers rightfully! After all, as we have seen, thousands of agricultural varieties of every color, taste, and size are disappearing or disappearing forever, replaced by the standardized seeds of large seed companies and multinationals.

Fortunately, in the last decades of the twentieth century, some groups of passionate horticulturists took care of the ancient seeds that survived the massacre. These heroes of biodiversity are known as seed savers, and there are more and more of them.

We must thank them that many varieties, now reduced to a flicker, were saved from extinction, reproduced, and finally redistributed to associations of passionate horticulturists. The largest is currently the American Seeds Savers' Exchange.

Up until a few years ago, the seed saver movement was still a niche phenomenon because few people still shared the idea of the importance of agricultural biodiversity and the need to return to the land and food sovereignty.

In recent times, the world of sustainable agriculture has been in great turmoil, and ancient seeds are regaining their place in society. By now, the countryside is no longer enough to contain the enthusiasm for the rediscovery of rural biodiversity: today, you can find gardens with ancient seeds even in urban centers!

Now that you know the value that your hands can help to create and build, therefore, my suggestion is that you pick up this book, re-read it several times, and put into practice all the advice, from the simplest to the most advanced, that I left you from my twenty years of experience.

Don't limit your desire to learn and contribute: the future of the Earth also depends on you!

I'm counting on you!

Manufactured by Amazon.ca
Acheson, AB